People Power

Jon Robins
with
Paul Stookes

People Power
by Jon Robins with Paul Stookes

© 2008 Lawpack Publishing
Lawpack Publishing Limited
76–89 Alscot Road
London SE1 3AW

www.lawpack.co.uk

All rights reserved
Printed in Great Britain

ISBN: 978-1-905261-59-8

The views expressed in this book are those of the authors and quoted sources and they do not represent the views of Lawpack Publishing Limited or of the *Daily Telegraph*.

Exclusion of Liability and Disclaimer

CONTENTS

ABOUT THE AUTHORS

Jon Robins, BA is an award-winning freelance journalist. For over ten years he has written about legal and consumer rights for the national and specialist press. He writes regularly for *The Observer* and *The Times*. He is also director for campaigns and communications at the Legal Action Group, a national charity which promotes equal access to justice for all. Until recently Jon edited *Independent Lawyer*, a monthly magazine for legal aid lawyers. He is also the author of *Affordable Law: How to get legal advice without breaking the bank* (Lawpack, 2004). In 2005 he won the Bar Council's legal reporter of the year.

Paul Stookes, MSc, LLB (Hons) Law, CEnv, MIEMA is a solicitor-advocate and partner at the law firm Richard Buxton, specialising in environmental and public law. He is the author of *A Practical Approach to Environmental Law* (OUP, 2005) and *Environmental Action: A guide for individuals and communities* (ELF, 2003). He is also a part-time senior lecturer in environmental and planning law at the School of Law, University of Hertfordshire. Paul has been a specialist adviser to the European Commission, the UNEP Global Judges Programme in Nairobi, and the government's Environmental Audit Committee's 2004/05 Inquiry: Environmental Crime. He was chief executive at the national charity the Environmental Law Foundation from 2001 to 2005 and is a member of the Law Society Council.

INTRODUCTION

This book is aimed at local grass roots campaigning groups. Whether you are trying to stop a much-loved playground being bulldozed and turned into a supermarket, fighting to improve the quality of school meals or trying to keep your local beach clean this is the book for you.

First of all, a brief explanation as to how the book was researched and written. Campaigning is about getting out there and taking action and that is how we approached the book. We interviewed campaigners, seasoned veterans and first-timers, about what works and what doesn't. To do this, we sent out the *People Power* questionnaire to groups involved in a wide range of campaigning activities over the summer of 2007.

The questionnaire is included in Appendix 1 and the groups that responded are listed on page xiv. We then followed up and interviewed those people involved in the running of such groups. We also interviewed professionals at national groups such as the National Council for Voluntary Organisations and Friends of the Earth who work with campaigners on a local level. This book is the sum of those experiences and offers practical advice on how to campaign effectively.

Many commentators have reflected upon the paradox of society's apparent disengagement from mainstream politics and a growing willingness to become involved in community-based actions and campaigning. Britain's democratic system is in crisis, claim the doomsayers. At first glance, the evidence doesn't look that promising. Turnout at the last two general elections (59% and 61%) has been the lowest since World War I and barely one-third of voters bother to go to the polls for local elections.

Have people really given up and retreated into apathy? Of course they haven't and *People Power* provides evidence that many people are convinced that they can bring about change in their own communities and beyond. This book documents the fact that campaigning groups can and do make a difference.

The campaigning spirit is alive and well. Intriguingly, recent research (by the Power Inquiry, chaired by Baroness Helena Kennedy, into political participation in Britain) found that even among the most politically disenfranchised (those who don't vote in general elections) more than one-third (37%) were members of or active in a charity, community or campaigning group. It was estimated that three out of five of us claim to have been somehow involved in the Make Poverty History campaign (nfpSynergy's *Campaigns and the Public Report*, 2006). The last few years have seen ordinary people out on the streets in unprecedented numbers – 1.5 million marching on Parliament to protest against the Iraq war in 2003 and 400,000 in the Liberty and Livelihood pro-hunting demonstration the year before.

At the time of researching *People Power*, the camp for climate change was in full force and was front page news. 'I'm going to get the message across that opposition to airports is anything but fringe,' Susan Kramer, the Liberal Democrat MP told the press. 'It comes from mainstream law-abiding residents who have suffered long enough. My constituents are not NIMBYs [as in Not In My Back Yard]. They live under the flight path.' No longer is eco-protest and direct action seen as the preserve of Swampy-style 'extremists'. It has gone mainstream.

Even the meaning of that pejorative acronym NIMBY, often unfairly invoked by the media against those perceived to be unnecessarily objecting to unwelcome development, has been revisited in recent years. 'The NIMBY is not the enemy of progress but its begetter,' championed one commentator (in the *New Statesman*, May 2004). 'In a land, and increasingly a world, where democracy is bought and where the global trumps the local every time, the NIMBYs – those prepared to defend what they know and love against the depredations of the distant and the disengaged – are the true heroes. It is they, not the house-builders and their tame ministers, who represent the best of what democracy is about.'

Not that any of the groups involved in this book would ever describe themselves by reference to that acronym. Many have gone out of their way to test that their campaigns reflect the wider concerns of the communities in which they live to head off such a charge. This book reflects a diverse range of causes and an equally varied array of campaigning styles. We speak to embattled families fighting to keep care homes open for their elderly relatives in Norfolk, to the residents of West Gateshead in the North East concerned about the impact of landfill on the environment, parents in London trying to improve the quality of food for their kids and a York-based campaigner trying to bring about a national ban on foie gras. Campaigns range from a one-man band run from a teenager's bedroom to groups with thousands of members worldwide.

But does campaigning make a difference? Absolutely.

People Power features many examples of local actions making real headway. Unsurprisingly, though, we found our campaigners in different states of mind. 'I do hope your book is going to tell the truth and not mislead people into believing in the cruel fallacy that the title suggests,' said one wearied activist involved in fighting care home closures. It was a sentiment expressed by a number of her colleagues engaged in the campaign in a lively email exchange to which we were made party. However, more often than not, responses were upbeat and the vast majority very positive. What became clear was that many campaigners felt emboldened by having the courage of their convictions to make a difference. 'I never realised I could make change happen – and it has made me braver about challenging other things,' said one.

We hope that you find this book helpful.

Jon Robins and Paul Stookes

ACKNOWLEDGEMENTS

Chapter 1

Thanks to Peter Dyer at Community Links, Bromley for his input on group organisation.

Chapter 2

We are grateful to Campaigning Effectiveness at the National Council for Voluntary Organisations (NCVO) for permission to use material from *The Good Campaigns Guide* (Kingham & Coe, NCVO, 2005), which we recommend for further reading on strategic thinking. In particular, thanks to Chris Stalker, head of Campaigning Effectiveness, for his input on this and other chapters.

Chapter 3

Nick Sladden from the accountants Baker Tilly advised us on the 'Handling Money' section of this chapter and we also appreciate the Institute of Fundraising for its contribution to both the 'Raising Money' sections (as well as the use of materials from the Institute's *Good Funding Guide*).

Chapter 4

The press team at Which? and Sue Stapely (www.suestapely.com), strategic communications consultant helped with their expertise on media in this chapter.

Chapter 5

We are grateful to the Corporate Responsibility Coalition and the Trade Justice Movement for allowing us to co-opt its *Act Now! A campaigner's guide to the Companies Act.* Thanks also to Vicki Fewkes for reading through and offering her views. We also appreciate the help of the Local Government Association, the Improvement and Development Agency for Local Government and the UK Office of the European Parliament.

Chapter 6

Paul Caplan, who runs Internationale (www.theinternationale.org), a company that helps charities and government with online campaigning, wrote much of this chapter. Thanks also to Jenny Lloyd of the Brighton-based IT specialists Nixon McInnes who also provided technical input.

Chapter 7

We are grateful to the Market Research Society and the freedom of information campaigner Heather Brooke (www.yrtk.org) for helping us with this chapter and for allowing us to use the model letters in Appendix 5.

Appendices

Thanks to Liberty for allowing us to use their *Guide to Peaceful Protest*, as well as to the publisher Pluto (www.plutobooks.com) for its permission.

Finally, Jon would like to say many, many thanks to Juliet, Bea and Eve. Paul would like to thank his family and colleagues for their support.

A very special thanks to everyone who has helped in our research for this book by completing the *People Power* questionnaire, answering our questions, providing guidance and expertise. In particular:

- Age Concern
- Alzheimer's Society
- Ban Foie Gras campaign
- Campaign to Protect Rural England
- Community Links, Bromley

- Demand Group
- Denholme Residents' Action Group
- Dump the Dump
- Environmental Law Foundation
- Friends of the Earth
- Gullivers Action Group
- Help the Aged
- Liberty
- Lydd Airport Action Group
- Merton Parents for Better Food
- Modbury Traders
- National Council for Voluntary Organisations
- Old Sodbury Compost Farm Action Group
- Pro-Test
- RAGE (Residents' Action Group for the Elderly)
- Residents for the Protection of Nidderdale
- Sheila McKechnie Foundation
- Stop Bristol Airport Expansion Coalition
- Surfers Against Sewage
- Tescopoly
- UK Pesticides Campaign
- Voluntary Action Sheffield
- Which?
- Xtraordinary People
- Your Right to Know

CHAPTER 1

Starting off

> 'Most campaigns tend to follow an initial spark of enthusiasm. There is an almost spontaneous need for change. To begin with the desire to remedy the problem is usually the campaign's driving force. After the initial response, it soon becomes clear that getting organised as quickly as possible is vital if you intend to maintain and pursue your campaign.'
>
> David Whiting, chief executive of the Environmental Law Foundation

Where to start? Your first instinct when embarking upon a campaign might well be to seek out like-minded people by, for example, holding a meeting. That instinct is a good one. Of course, there is strength in numbers but there are other compelling reasons for testing how others feel about an issue. If you are leading local action, then you need to be able to demonstrate your legitimacy to speak on behalf of others. Do you really represent the interests of the community you are holding yourself out to? Never assume that everyone feels as strongly as you do. Test the waters.

The theme of much of this chapter is striking a balance between keeping your group informal and the imposing structures which might improve the ability of the group to do its job but which inevitably detract from its main aims. Issues to do with group democracy (e.g. how you make decisions) and delegation of work within a group (e.g. who does what) cause problems unless you have clear structures in place from the start.

> pass over

If you choose to keep your group simple in structure, then there are very few formal rules when it comes to setting up and running an effective campaign. You can run your campaign as a one-man band from your bedroom via the Internet, or alternatively you could become a company limited by guarantee with charitable status. The degree of formality is a matter for you.

For any group starting up, once you join with others to fight a common cause you should ensure that everyone is clear about the aims of the campaign and what is required of each member of the group. Working as a group provides a source of mutual support and ideas, as well as bringing in resources and sharing the campaign workload. It also demonstrates collective and united action, but big campaigns need greater organisation with group structures and decision-making procedures which must be well-defined and understood by the whole group.

When you are starting off you need to think about what form your group should take. How are you going to arrive at key decisions? A consistent theme from campaigners that took part in the *People Power* questionnaire (see Appendix 1) was the benefits delivered by simplicity.

You need to ask yourself the following basic questions:

Big or small...what do you want to be?

'We aren't a charity; we aren't even "an organisation" with a memorandum or articles of association. We're just a small project that doesn't need any money. In fact, it's just me, the website with some video clips, and an email list. That's all you need,' says Paul Blanchard, a Labour councillor in York who runs the Ban Foie Gras campaign. His 'group' is very much a one-man band, but in the space of three months in 2007 it generated a huge amount of press coverage.

Some groups that responded to the *People Power* questionnaire were backed by thousands of paying supporters, raised considerable amounts of money through events and merchandise, and adopted formal business structures. 'We started off as a local campaign in 1990 with the aim of cleaning up two beaches – St Agnes and Porthtowan,' explains Andy Cummins, campaigns officer at Surfers Against Sewage. 'We now have in the region of 8,000 paying members. We are a limited company, but a non-profit-making one. We have a board of directors, but they are all volunteers, they don't take a wage and so all the money goes straight into the campaign.' How does the group perceive itself – as a business, or as an environmental campaigning group? 'The campaigning comes first,' he replies. 'Everything – all the profits go back into the organisation and the campaign is the most important thing.'

How do you make decisions?

'We have a steering group of 12 to 15 members,' explains Jackie Schneider, who set up Merton Parents for Better Food in April 2005 to improve the quality of school food. 'But to be honest – and I know this sounds a bit Stalinist – I admit I have an undue influence. I worked in a school, know how the system works and had done tons of research. Together with Chris (a school governor who chaired the first meeting), we make the decisions.'

Being united behind a cause doesn't mean the campaigning will be without headaches, clashing egos and internal bickering. One veteran campaigner notes wearily, 'too much talking, not enough doing – that's probably the best way to summarise the last five years of our intermittent fighting. Our little group succeeded as a social and talking club, but did it make a difference?'

Our tip is to plan ahead.

3

Testing the waters

If you are just starting out and your fledgling campaign comprises you plus a couple of kindred spirits, then you might want to test the strength of feeling in your community and beyond. Before proceeding too far, check to see whether there are any other local or national groups campaigning for or concerned about the same issues as your group. If there are, you should contact them and, if appropriate, join forces.

The question on your lips at this stage is most likely to be, 'Does anybody out there feel like we do?' There is one sure-fire way to find out and that is to arrange an informal meeting at either someone's home, the local village hall or local pub. Set a date, contact your neighbours and ask them to come along. Consider printing a small, A5-size flyer to deliver through doors (see the example on page 6). You may want to telephone or email people as a further reminder. Set out your concerns concisely and make sure all basic information (e.g. date, time and venue) is included. Also, ask people to reply to let you know whether they are attending. If someone can't make a meeting, you should nevertheless see whether they are interested in working with the group and ask whether it is OK for you to keep them informed.

It's essential to ensure that you have the names and contact details of everyone interested in joining the group. Jackie Schneider kick-started her influential school dinners campaign, Merton Parents for Better Food, by writing to every head teacher in the borough and

How much time people will not to comma

asking them to send the letter to all their governors. It followed shortly after TV chef Jamie Oliver had raised the nation's awareness about the poor quality of food in schools, not to mention the horror of turkey twizzlers. 'About 150 people turned up at our first meeting,' she says. 'I had prepared a slip of paper so they could put their name on it, the school they were involved with, their role and contact number and what their concern was. Those slips of paper were crucial and without them it would have just been a wonderful meeting – that would have been it.'

Circulate a contacts sheet for people to complete (see page 7). At the end of your initial meeting, explain what your next steps are. For the 100 New Homes example (below), this could be to arrange a meeting at your local council's planning department to discuss the proposal with planning officers. You should also arrange a further group meeting for those members of the community who are happy to help out. It might be useful to propose that, even at this early stage, it is likely that the campaign will be based upon a working group with a small committee that carries out specific functions but that everyone else is welcome to join as members. In this way, it will be possible to carry on manageable group meetings that can be held in someone's home and so avoid the need for organising venues, etc. This is discussed in the following section.

You need to consider how you want to use your support. For example, Merton Parents for Better Food formed a steering group of 15 members from those who attended the first meeting; although Jackie Schneider points out that she, together with a school governor, Chris Larkham, who chaired that first meeting, makes the day-to-day decisions. Members may be limited to those with a designated task or elected as the officers of the management committee. Alternatively, you could have a large number that generally support the campaign but are not otherwise actively involved. You will see that the example constitution at Appendix 2 regards members as anyone interested in helping the group to achieve its purpose or objectives, willing to abide by the rules of the group and willing to pay a subscription agreed by the management committee. That is one model of running a group but, clearly, not

100 NEW HOMES ON THE VILLAGE GREEN

Redbrick builders have applied to build 100 executive homes on the village green.

There is a meeting for local residents to discuss this on:

Tuesday 18th April at 7.30 pm
Venue: The Village Hall

ALL WELCOME!

(please let me know whether or not you are able to attend).

For more information please call Joe Bloggs on 01234 567 890 or e-mail j.bloggs@group-mail.com

appropriate for many small-scale groups. Many groups prefer to keep it simple. The simplest way to know who your members and supporters are is to keep updated a membership database. This may be done on a spreadsheet which can hold all contact details, information on subscription fees and any donations, or, for example, whether they have any expertise that may assist the group (see below).

Remember that any information held on a group database is confidential and should not be disclosed. The Data Protection Act 1998 requires all organisations to protect personal information against unauthorised use and accidental loss. Ensure that someone in your campaign group is responsible for managing any personal database. This could be the campaign secretary (see later). Whoever you nominate to look after personal databases, ensure that they fully understand the group's obligations in protecting personal information. The Information Commissioner's Office provides helpful information on holding and obtaining personal information. In November 2007 it published a *Data Protection Good*

Model Contacts Sheet

NAME	ADDRESS	TEL	EMAIL	DO YOU WANT TO JOIN WORKING GROUP?	ANY PARTICULAR EXPERIENCE/ EXPERTISE?	WILLING TO PROVIDE GENERAL SUPPORT?

Practice Note: Security of personal information for small and medium sized organizations outlining the security measures groups should have in place to protect the personal information they hold (www.ico.gov.uk).

For more information on holding meetings, see chapter 4.

Building alliances

At the outset of the chapter it was recommended that one of the first things that a new group should do is seek out like-minded groups and allies. Campaigning works most effectively through coalitions, alliances and networks. You can learn from the experiences of others, share resources plus build momentum for your own cause through working with others. Tescopoly (www.tescopoly.org), an alliance of different groups which highlights the environmental and social impact of the supermarket giant, is a good example of this.

The Tescopoly Alliance includes a diverse range of groups from Banana Link (a UK group working towards a fair and sustainable banana trade), Friends of the Earth, GMB London, the Small and Family Farms Alliance, through to anti-poverty groups such as War on Want. It also includes details of a large number of local campaign groups on its site plus resources for would-be campaigners. Tescopoly is not an organisation in its own right. 'It works around a coalition of organisations that links people in the UK such as those who are fighting to protect their high street or small farmers who are having extravagant demands placed upon them by the likes of Tesco to, for example, overseas suppliers in the wine industry in South Africa or the conditions of fruit pickers,' explains Owen Espley, corporate power campaigner at Friends of the Earth. 'In that sense, you build a coalition which takes head-on the company in all its different activities. For the smaller groups, I find that it helps create a platform or a way in to amplify their issues by linking themselves to a wider campaign.'

When seeking out alliances don't just think of other local groups;

Model Membership Database Form

A	B	C	D	E	F	G	H	I
		YOUR CAMPAIGN		MEMBERS' DATABASE				
NAME	SURNAME	ADDRESS	POST CODE	TEL	EMAIL	SUBSCRIPTIONS	DONATIONS	EXPERTISE
Chris	Smith	145 The Street Any Town	AT45 2LP	01234 567890	csmith@email.co.uk	£10	£0	-
Peter	Johnson	13 The Street Anytown	AT14 9KL	01234 567890	peterj@email.co.uk	£10	£10	surveyor
						£10	£0	
						£10	£0	
						£10	£0	
						£10	£0	
						£10	£0	

also consider approaching other organisations, from trade unions to consumer groups and professional bodies.

There are practical issues to consider about joint campaigning. There are clear advantages to be had from improved economies of scale such as a greater skills-base and increased resources and audience. However, the structures discussed throughout the chapter need to be applied to the larger group.

You need to be clear about what is expected from your partner campaign groups. Do you want to share information? At the very least, you should be mindful of their campaign timetable and events. Perhaps you might want to go further and sign up to joint aims and objectives.

Group structure

Getting organised and working as a group need not be overwhelming or overly complex, but you do need to be clear about how your campaign will be managed.

Where to start? 'Running a group is very much a team effort – you can't do it alone! It isn't only about the amount of work that you have to do, it is also about shared responsibility,' says Peter Dyer at Community Links, Bromley, a local group that supports campaigners. 'To begin with you should just bring together people who share similar interests and concerns. Work out what your main aims are and how you think you will achieve them. In our experience, groups usually begin with about three or four people who soon realise that setting up a group involves a great deal of work and that things will probably be made easier if you can bring in others to assist.'

You will need to think, quite early on, about how your group will be structured and managed. You will need to sort out practical things such as the level of commitment you might expect from members, how often you need to meet and where. You will also need to be clear as to who does what, why and when. Do you expect to be handling money? What if you expect to receive donations? These financial considerations are dealt with in chapter 3.

As for the basics, Peter Dyer says, 'two fundamental things that all groups should have in place from the very start are a management committee and a set of rules which the group complies with.' These rules are also known as the constitution.

Your campaign may well start out (and, indeed, run quite happily) as an informal group of just two or three people. It could also evolve into a larger, more formal organisation. There is no optimum size for a campaign group. As said earlier, it doesn't follow that 'bigger is better'. It might be that your objectives are more easily achieved as a small campaign with a lot of supporters rather than being a bigger campaign including a lot of members with, inevitably, differing levels of commitment and different views on what your objectives are. For instance, the UK Pesticides Campaign (www.pesticides campaign.co.uk), which highlights the high level of pesticide exposure for people living in agricultural areas, is largely run by one prominent campaigner, Georgina Downs. She has put the issue on the national agenda and taken legal action against the government over its absence of any risk assessment relating to crop-spraying. Compare this with, say, the Campaign to Protect Rural England (CPRE), which has over 60,000 members and 200 district groups and runs a number of campaigns on matters as diverse as hedgerows, tranquillity and light pollution. Each organisation runs effective campaigns but is different in terms of scale, number of members and resources.

'Our campaign has many thousands of supporters from not only here in the UK, but also from around the world and provides a voice for millions of people who live close to fields that are regularly sprayed with pesticides as a result of the intensification of agricultural production methods and dependence on pesticide use,' explains Georgina Downs of the UK Pesticides Campaign. 'However, it suits us to have an informal group structure that can be flexible, and allows us to say what needs to be said without having to compromise the campaign's position [which might happen] if there is a large organisational structure in place.' She adds, 'We feel strongly in our campaign and think it's important to be able to say what we want, when we want, in order to achieve the necessary changes to give rural residents and others the high level of protection from pesticides that they have the right to expect.'

You have options as to the type of group you wish to form. In fact, one paper (*Governance and Organisational Structures, Governance Hub/Co-operatives UK*, 2007) lists ten different types. By far the most common structure for grass roots local campaigns is the 'unincorporated association'. Limited companies and charities might be appropriate for the bigger and more established groups.

One type of group model is not necessarily 'better' than the other. You must decide what is right for you at the present time. If you want to adopt a different structure at a later stage, then this is always possible as part of your general review of the campaign.

If you and your fellow campaigners have already embarked upon a common enterprise with a basic understanding of your mutual obligations and how money will be dealt with, then you are in an 'unincorporated association', whether you are aware of that or not.

Most residents' associations, community groups and local action groups will be unincorporated associations. You do not have to register or obtain any licence to operate. An unincorporated association does not have a separate legal identity, which means that any liability for the group's actions rests with you, the members. Further, as an unincorporated association, your group is unable to enter into any formal legal contracts in its own name. On the other hand, an incorporated group, such as a limited company, does have a legal identity and there is protection from personal liability.

This arrangement might suit you fine. You might not consider anything more than the most informal structure. The absence of bureaucracy means you can get on with the job in hand – which is running a campaign. You aren't required to formally register or seek regulatory approval for a change in your corporate objectives as is necessary for a limited company.

Paul Blanchard of Ban Foie Gras sees discussions of group structures as irrelevant. 'You don't need anything more than yourself,' he says. 'You don't need money and you don't need staff for our kind of guerrilla campaigning. It's different now – we are campaigning in the age of the Internet.'

Many activists do not think in organisational terms at first. However, as your campaign evolves, there will be issues that have to be dealt with. 'When we first started it was all about me and my ability to campaign knowing that I had the national dyslexia charities behind me,' says Kate Griggs, who set up Xtraordinary People to raise awareness and funding to support dyslexia training in schools. In two years, this one-woman campaign has turned into a charitable initiative which at the end of 2007 received a government pump-priming grant of nearly £1 million for a two-year period to kick-start a particular initiative with a commitment to match that pound for pound. 'And that is very daunting,' she adds.

Before you begin your campaign you should check if there are any other groups that might share your concerns, such as:

- **Residents' associations and community groups.** In other words, other locals might already be involved in an unincorporated group, which they use, for example, to hold an annual community festival or to co-ordinate a neighbourhood watch scheme. If a different concern arises locally, it may well be that your residents' association is a good forum to air it and the association may agree to pursue the campaign and then rely on the existing association as a ready-made group to put the campaign into action. It is therefore important for you to check at the outset whether your local residents' association wishes to campaign on the same issue. If so, the group is ready-made. If not, then at least you know that you will not be unnecessarily duplicating any work being carried on by others.

- **Amenity or civic societies.** An amenity or civic society group will often be more formal and perhaps larger than a residents' association or community group. They have a general role in the locality promoting high standards of planning, conservation and regeneration in their local community. Again, it is always worth checking with the local civic or amenity society for their views on your campaign. According to the Civic Trust (the national umbrella body for 850 local groups) civic societies are voluntary local organisations which undertake practical projects, including restoring old buildings, improving the quality of public places and finding solutions to traffic problems. The Civic Trust website, www.civictrust.org.uk, notes that civic societies have a formal role as community watchdogs commenting on planning applications for new buildings and developments and guarding against unsympathetic changes to conservation areas and historic buildings.

Limited company

Running your group as a limited company can have advantages. Non-profit-making companies tend to be run as a company limited by guarantee; this is broadly the same as a conventional limited company but without shareholders or shares. Instead, it will have trustees or guarantors who guarantee to pay an agreed sum (often just £1) if the company is wound up. A limited company is a legal entity, or 'person', in its own right which can then enter into contracts or make public comment or statements – in other words, in the company's name rather than in the names of the individuals that run it. As a result, any financial risk will be limited to the extent of the guaranteed amount provided by the guarantors, for example £1 per trustee. Moreover, any legal liability that could arise – for example, by making a libellous statement – would be the company's liability rather than the members of your campaign group.

Andy Cummins is one of six permanent staff at Surfers Against Sewage, which has 6,000 to 8,000 supporters. He describes the group as 'hard hitting' and 'operating outside of the doors of power and not afraid of naming and shaming people'. He says that one reason for being a limited company is that 'if somebody decided to take us to court it would be pretty unfair on the six of us, considering all the extra work we put in, to then be fined for the actions of one of our supporters'.

One extreme illustration of the risk to campaigners is what befell the two defendants in the infamous McLibel trial, in which two members of London Greenpeace were sued for libel in their own names by McDonald's for publishing and distributing concerns about the food group's operations. The ensuing legal action between the food giant and two self-styled anarchists became the longest legal action in the British courts lasting two-and-a-half years. It generated 18,000 pages of court transcripts and 40,000 pages of documents. In fact, it turned out to be a spectacular own goal for McDonald's because it generated acres of negative press giving the issues more prominence than the campaigners could have had hoped, plus McDonald's was cast as an overbearing Goliath to the campaigner's fearless David. The legacy of McLibel appears to be that pressure groups tend not to get sued for libel because of the reputational risk.

Another advantage of being a limited company is that you can limit your personal exposure to legal costs if you consider pursuing a legal action. For example, if your campaign group as a company sued a government department and ultimately lost your case, the government's legal costs would have to be paid by the company rather than your individual group members (this is discussed in chapter 8).

The downside of limited companies is that valuable time will have to be spent on paperwork as well as precious money diverted in compliance costs. There are various statutory duties that a company has under the Companies Act. You are required to file accounts and company returns (basic updated information about the company) within ten months of the accounting year under Companies House rules and you will have to file changes of directors and secretary with Companies House. Companies also have to comply with formal rules about holding meetings and consulting with shareholders if appropriate. Directors who are responsible for the management of a company have certain formal obligations. It is likely that one or more key members of your campaign group will also be company officers; for example, your group chair could also be the company managing director, the group secretary could be the company secretary and so on. Having said that, it is not difficult to set up a limited company (not least if you can draw on the skills of a lawyer or accountant who supports the group), but the benefits of limiting your liability must outweigh the time and effort involved in the administration. You could set up your company through a company formation agent for as little as £50. On top of that the annual return filing fee is £30 – check out the Companies House website, www.companieshouse.gov.uk.

Charitable trusts

Groups that provide a general public benefit can often register themselves as a charity. There are some, mainly financial, advantages in being a charity.

The Charities Act 2006 requires a charity to have one or more purposes which fall within a list of 13 descriptions including:

- the prevention or relief of poverty;

- the advancement of education;

- the advancement of religion;

- the advancement of health or the saving of lives;

- the advancement of citizenship or community development;

- the advancement of the arts, culture, heritage or science;

- the advancement of amateur sport;

- the advancement of human rights, conflict resolution or reconciliation or the promotion of religious or racial harmony or equality and diversity;

- the advancement of environmental protection or improvement;

- the relief of those in need, by reason of youth, age, ill-health, disability, financial hardship or other disadvantage;

- the advancement of animal welfare;

- the promotion of the efficiency of the armed forces of the Crown or of the police, fire and rescue services or ambulance services; or

- other purposes currently recognised as charitable and any new charitable purposes which are similar to another charitable purpose.

A charity also has to ensure that the charitable purpose will benefit the public and this will depend on the circumstances of the nature of the purpose itself. It is the Charity Commission that will assess whether the charitable purposes set by the organisation will benefit the public. The public benefit requirement and the provisions on charitable purposes are due to come into force on 1 April 2008.

However, a charity cannot have some charitable purposes and some that are not. It may be that part of your campaign's work could be defined as having a charitable purpose. If so, you could set up a separate charitable trust alongside the main campaign group and any charitable work carried out could benefit from its charitable trust status.

The advantages and disadvantages of being a charity are set out below. If you want to register as a charity, your group must fall within the list of 13 descriptions above, be for the public benefit and have an income of over £5,000 per annum. There are then a number of options:

- **Unincorporated charitable trust.** You would set the organisation up under a trust deed. Provided that you were accepted as being a charity, you would be regulated by the Charity Commission and group members would be trustees and subject to the requirements of the Charity Act 1993. This is the simplest form of charity structure but it doesn't offer any protection as regards personal liability (see below). You are individual trustees and potentially liable for, among other things, any of the unincorporated charity's debts or legal actions.

- **Charity as a company limited by guarantee.** You are creating a company and then registering it with the Charity Commission. You immediately have the protection of limited liability.

- **Charitable Incorporated Organisation (CIO).** This type of organisation was introduced under the Charities Act 2006 and will be available from 2008 onwards. The idea behind the CIO is to have something that will be recognised as a separate legal entity like a company but without the same burdensome regulation. CIOs will be regulated by the Charity Commission, avoiding the dual regulation of charitable companies, which report to both Companies House and the Charity Commission. They will have limited liability.

Should you register as a charity?

Advantages of being a charity:

- you don't normally have to pay Income/Corporation Tax, Capital Gains Tax, or Stamp Duty, and gifts to charities are free of Inheritance Tax;

- tax relief is available to those who give to charity, which is a powerful incentive for businesses and individuals alike to donate to your cause;

- you pay no more than 20% of normal business rates on the charity's buildings;

- you can get special VAT treatment in some circumstances;

- you are often able to raise funds from the public, grant-making trusts and local government more easily than non-charitable bodies;

- you can formally represent and help to meet the needs of the community; and

- you can give the public greater reassurance that the organisation is regulated because it is monitored by the Charity Commission.

Disadvantages of being a charity:

- you must have 'exclusively' charitable purposes. Some organisations may have a range of activities, some charitable, some not. To become a charity an organisation would have to stop its non-charitable activities (see over);

- you will have limits on the extent of political campaigning activity you can carry on;

- strict rules apply to trading carried out by charities;

- trustees are not allowed to receive financial benefits (e.g. salaries, or business contracts to a trustee's own business) from the charity unless specifically authorised by the governing document (e.g. constitution); and

- charity law imposes certain financial reporting obligations. These vary with the size of the charity.

There is an uneasy relationship between the narrow constraints of charity law and the desire on the part of groups to campaign and many groups would like to see a more liberal regime. The traditional line is vehemently opposed to the idea of charities being too political – as said above, a disadvantage of being a charity is you cannot be political; however, increasingly charities and campaigning groups have found the law overly restrictive. This latter view has come into recent focus with the advisory group on campaigning and the voluntary sector, chaired by Baroness Helena Kennedy QC, which made the case for a relaxation of the restriction on the amount of political campaigning charities can do. At the time of going to press, the government has promised to review the Charity Commission guidance, CC9 – Political Activities and Campaigning by Charities. Key to this debate is an interpretation of the law that says political activity must not become the 'dominant' means by which a charity carries out its purposes and must remain 'ancillary'. Campaigning groups are worried that the rule disadvantages small charities. The government appears to favour relaxing the rules and said in the review that 'it is surely possible, in a well-run charity, for political activity to be "dominant" within a charity and yet still enable it to further its charitable purposes'.

The Charity Commission, responding to concerns that charities were being overly cautious, published advice on how (as they put it) they can 'follow the example of successful campaigns like the Make Poverty History coalition and the RSPCA's controversial campaign on fox-hunting and use their unique position in society to fight for change'. Its advice came out in April 2007. Andrew Hind, Chief Executive of the Charity Commission, said, 'Campaigning, advocacy and political activities can all be legitimate and valuable activities for charities to undertake. In fact the strong links charities have in their local communities, the high levels of public trust and confidence they command, and the diversity of causes they represent, mean that charities are often uniquely placed to campaign and advocate on behalf of their beneficiaries.'

Many smaller groups, particularly local groups, don't tend to seriously consider becoming a charity. Many are deterred by the perceived bureaucracy. Xtraordinary People operates as 'a restricted fund' of the British Dyslexia Association, as Kate Griggs explains: 'In other words, we don't have our own charity name and number. We use that of the parent charity, the British Dyslexia Association. But any money that we raise goes into a restricted pot and that is governed by the national charity. It gives us the freedom of being able to raise money as a charity without the bureaucracy of the charity. Of course, that element is governed by the Charity Commission, which is as it should be.'

Surfers Against Sewage is also contemplating taking charitable status in light of the new Charities Act 2006. 'Until recently there have been so many restrictions on what charities can say and how they can campaign,' says Andy Cummins. 'We haven't wanted to compromise our ability to campaign for the price of getting more grants. But the laws are changing whereby environmental non-governmental organisations can obtain charitable status, so we would be able to apply for a lot more grants, and that would be fantastic.'

National organisations such as the National Council for Voluntary Organisations (NCVO), the Governance Hub (www.governance hub.org.uk) and VolResource (www.volresource.org.uk) provide information, advice and support for people setting up and working in the voluntary sector.

For more information on registering a charity, see the Charity Commission website, www.charity-commission.gov.uk.

Constitution

It is advisable for a campaign group, whatever structure you choose to adopt, to have a written document that sets out the aims and objectives. You will find an example of a model constitution at Appendix 2.

A limited company must adopt its own 'memorandum of association', which is a document recording the objects and powers of a company in its dealings with outsiders. A limited company must also have articles of association, which are, effectively, the by-laws of your group which cover its internal rules. A charity must have a constitution that sets out its charitable objectives. There is, by way of contrast, no legal requirement for an unincorporated association to adopt a formal set of rules or constitution, although it is wise to have one. It is a valuable discipline to articulate what you and your supporters want to achieve.

At the very least, you should make sure that your constitution sets out:

- the name of your group;
- your aims;
- the committee members;
- membership details; and
- rules regarding subscriptions, the holding of money and property, etc.

On occasions, it may well be necessary for the committee, or one of its officers, to take decisions on behalf of the group through executive powers. The model constitution at Appendix 2 does not provide for any delegated decision-making. It might be appropriate to insert a clause for delegated authority before the constitution is adopted (or it might be voted on and approved by the group at the AGM or a special meeting). A typical delegated authority clause is set out in the model constitution at clause 14 of Appendix 2.

Who does what

Right from the start you need to allocate tasks according to your members' strengths. We have just talked about the importance of having a set of rules (or constitution) to govern a group and which should define roles within the group. The type of work required by a campaign will vary. We have summarised the main tasks and cross-referenced to other chapters that deal with the topic in more detail.

Make use of your own talent. Take any cross-section of society and there might be a fair share of accountants or financially competent people who are well-placed to be a treasurer; IT specialists who can take charge of the website; and journalists who can become your press officers. Your group might have the support of business professionals – accountants, financial advisers and lawyers – who will be able to advise on particular issues. Their input will be very useful. Also be mindful that their natural instinct might be risk-averse and they might want to formalise arrangements and introduce legal structures. If there is a pressing need for work to be carried out but no experience in the group, then finding a willing new member/committee officer becomes a campaign priority.

The main roles in any campaign group are:

- **Chair.** Every group should have a leader who is prepared to take executive decisions or have a casting vote. There will be occasions when they will need to take decisions in a delegated capacity; for example, instructing a transport consultant to carry out an independent traffic assessment. The chair will also represent your group at meetings and will be the public voice (these tasks are identified in the example constitution). It could be that a new chair is elected at the Annual General Meeting (AGM) as, again, outlined in the constitution. These are issues to be considered from the start. It would be entirely appropriate to re-elect the same chair. However, it will be important to ensure that the opportunity for change is in place (e.g. by annual elections).

- **Treasurer.** Having a campaign treasurer is essential. It is likely that someone in the group will have some experience of dealing with finances or money. If so, they should feel comfortable about managing the campaign funds, at least in the early stages. However, you must be clear about the treasurer's role, and how much control or power they have over the group's finances. Their basic duties are set out in the constitution. It may also be helpful to draft a brief job description or terms of appointment for the treasurer. See chapter 3.

- **Administrator/committee secretary.** Good administration is essential in bigger groups. Important administrative tasks include ensuring that meetings (public and private) are well-organised and take place according to plan. This may include booking rooms, finalising speakers, and arranging for any equipment (including tables and chairs) to be available. Other important matters will include ensuring that meeting agendas, reports and minutes are available when appropriate (see below).

- **Campaign-specific tasks.** You are likely to have a number of tasks that will be specific to your campaign; for example, preventing the demolition of an historic building might need input from a dedicated conservation officer. A proposal to build a new road is likely to require evidence of traffic assessment on existing roads. It may well be that as part of your campaign you will have to instruct expert consultants to support it. Even so, you will still need a group member/officer to gather, analyse and refine the group's concerns in order to properly instruct your chosen expert.

You might also consider the following office-holders:

- Press officer: see chapter 4
- Government liaison officer: see chapter 5
- Website/IT officer: see chapter 6
- Information and research officer: see chapter 7

Decision-making

'There was some strife at the start over decision-making. I do recall voting on how to vote. When you get to that point you do realise that you have to streamline and – to put it politely – one or two people dropped out,' recalls Tom Holder, of Pro-Test, the Oxford-based campaign group in favour of animal testing and in support of scientific research.

It is important for you to sort out an approach to decision-making at an early stage. The model constitution in Appendix 2 provides for the group to be managed or administered by a management committee with a certain number of individuals elected at the group's AGM. This makes sense, even if your group only includes two or three members at present. A management committee can take decisions on behalf of the group and members of that committee can be elected to their posts.

Your group's management committee should have at least three officers: a chair, treasurer and a secretary (see above). A management committee of anything between three and nine officers is sensible.

All members of your group that are not officers of the management committee should nevertheless be entitled to vote for any matters that arise at the group's AGM or any special meeting that is arranged by the committee. However, the types of matters voted for at an AGM will be limited to important matters (e.g. electing officers of the committee).

Rallying the troops

Campaigning is time-consuming and requires stamina. It is essential to build and maintain an enthusiastic and committed team. Many campaign tasks could easily keep a full-time employee busy, but you won't have that luxury. If you are taking on an opponent such as a developer or government department, they will have the financial resources and staff to try to undermine your campaign. Of course, they won't have your commitment, nor will they have – as one campaigner puts it – 'our bloody-minded belief that we're right and they're rubbish'.

As your campaign grows it is vital to ensure that all members are kept fully informed and that their interest and enthusiasm remains alive. Publishing a regular newsletter, distributed by email, is one of the most efficient means of circulating information.

Another way to keep the momentum going with your campaign is to hold regular meetings to which all members are invited. See chapter 4.

So what does keep campaigning going? Denholme Residents' Action Group (DRAG) was set up in January 1999 to represent the people of Denholme, near Bradford, who were fighting a planning application to use a local quarry for a landfill site. Residents were concerned about air pollution, smell and noise. They did not want to live next to a rubbish dump for the next generation or two.

For nine years DRAG has represented residents at a planning inquiry and supported two High Court legal challenges, including one that went to the Court of Appeal. 'One major source of motivation has been the continuing suspect manoeuvres by the operators. This has angered us and anger is a very good motivator,' says Sharon Makinson, campaign secretary. 'At times, however, the campaign has gone at a very fast pace, such as when we needed to issue legal proceedings in the High Court within a short space of time. Many times it has been the adrenalin that has kept us going (and coffee!).'

CHAPTER 2

Strategy

> 'Campaigners are most successful when they combine strategic astuteness and tactical opportunism. The best campaigners make this look deceptively simple.'
>
> Campaigning Effectiveness at the National Council for Voluntary Organisations

If you are reading this book, the likelihood is that you will have some experience of campaigning. So from that experience you know that campaigns are driven by passion and enthusiasm. Seasoned campaigners will quickly say, yes, passion and enthusiasm are essential but the other ingredient that makes a campaign effective is planning.

When respondents to the *People Power* questionnaire (see Appendix 1) were asked about how they developed a campaign strategy, many admitted to struggling with the idea of planning. Some even resisted the notion. 'We are about doing and not talking,' said one campaigner. 'We all volunteer our time. Time's a precious commodity and so when we meet, it tends to be after work at someone's house. The time and energy that we have to commit to the cause is limited and when we do get involved we don't want it to become a talking shop.' Admirable maybe, but if you were to run a business on that basis, you would be bust in no time at all.

You need to channel the creative energy to power your group.

Campaigners want to 'do'; achieve change. What they don't want to do is 'sit around drinking endless cups of coffee talking about doing' (as another respondent puts it). But action for action's sake isn't enough, and it is likely to be a waste of scarce resources like time and money.

This chapter sets out general planning principles which apply whether you are trying to save the planet or the playground at the end of the road. 'Our philosophy of campaigning is that the same principles operate regardless of context and whether you are part of an international organisation trying to influence the policies of the World Bank and the IMF or a local campaign in Cambridge,' says Chris Stalker, head of Campaigning Effectiveness at the National Council for Voluntary Organisations (NCVO). 'You need to choose the right issues, build up a strong evidence base, be clear about what you want to achieve, focus your energies and resources on the right targets and build alliances.' His experience is that a lot of creative energy is wasted through a lack of strategic thinking.

Applying a discipline to strategic thinking (as opposed to being merely intuitive about your approach to campaigning) might seem artificial but there are many good reasons for doing it. It puts your consideration of the issues in a tried and tested framework, challenges your own assumptions and ensures you consider other options. The techniques that we cover in this chapter are often conventional management tools which have been pioneered (by the likes of NCVO) in campaigns of all sizes. We recommend them because they work.

> **CHAPTER OVERVIEW:**
> * Planning for impact
> * The campaign cycle

Planning for impact

The NCVO explains the mechanics of campaigning by reference to what it calls an 'impact chain' which breaks down 'the process of change into component parts'.

A simple model is as follows:

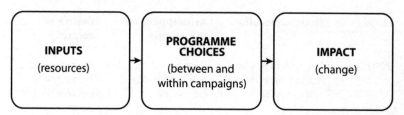

This basic structure breaks down even further, distinguishing between different levels of change:

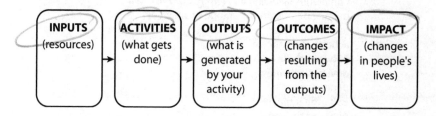

The point of the impact chain is that it helps you understand the components of an effective campaign. It also makes the point that campaigning is about making choices. Make the right choice and it will achieve the desired impact; whereas if you make the wrong choice you risk wasting your time and your money and that of other people.

A long-term campaign is all about exercising choice. Do you want to organise a press conference to launch your new report? Or is your time better spent on a mail-out to supporters asking them to write to their MP asking them to read the report?

This distinction between 'outputs' and 'outcomes' is critical. Campaigners tend to concentrate on the former – spending hours organising public meetings, holding press conferences, etc. The questions you should be asking are: 'What are the outcomes of this activity? What is the result of what we're doing? Are we achieving an impact?'

Understanding the impact chain

Stage	Short explanation	Assumptions in the process	Degree of control
INPUTS	The resources you put in – time, money and expertise	Certain resources are needed for your campaign	Your planned work; within internal control
ACTIVITIES	What you actually do with the available resources. Campaigns involving a mixture of lobbying, media and other actions. The balance between these different activities depends on the issue, the ultimate goal and the context	If you have access to these resources then you can use them to accomplish a range of activities	
OUTPUTS	Your actions measured and monitored. For example, X number of meetings with ministers and officials; Y thousands of signatures on a petition; amount of media coverage	If you accomplish these activities, you will deliver a certain set of results	
OUTCOMES	The milestones of change. Impact will be your final goal but the outcomes plot the steps along the way in the short term; this might involve, for example, parts of the media taking up your issue or a government spokesperson issuing a public statement (even if it is not supportive of your goals).	If you deliver these results, then you will help to achieve change in the ways that certain parts of the public or institutions regard a particular issue and how they behave in relation to it...	Your intended results; subject to increasing external influence

	In the longer term you could see the government taking steps to change the way legislation is being enacted		
IMPACT	How have things changed as a result of your campaign? What are the significant or lasting changes in people's lives to which your actions have contributed? How do they affect others?	If you achieve these changes, benefits will accrue to those whom you represent	Your intended results; subject to increasing external influence

The idea behind this model of campaign strategy is that it ensures that you do not concentrate all your energies on 'outputs'. You can organise a demo and march through the streets of London, but if you are merely thinking about the 'output' (i.e. numbers of people) there might not be an 'outcome' in terms of effect and therefore no subsequent impact.

The campaign cycle

The impact chain is a way of explaining how change happens. It is to help you understand the overall principles that campaigning is based on, and to help you make choices to achieve impact. The 'campaign cycle' is what NCVO calls 'a planning tool' to help you think through the different ways to make an impact.

THE CAMPAIGN CYCLE

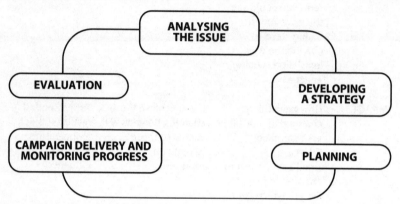

The campaign cycle emphasises the concept of campaigning as an integrated process which moves from the start (e.g. understanding the issue) to the finish (e.g. evaluation) and then back to the start again. As such it offers a framework for planning your campaign and keeps you on track.

Analysing the issue

Understanding the issue

In your own mind you will have a grasp of the issues at stake, but you need to communicate your concerns to others – policy-makers, supporters and funders. Don't assume that all members of your group will be singing from the same hymn sheet. People respond to the same problem in different ways and you need to establish exactly what your group stands for.

'The crucial thing we did at the early stages was establish our aims and objectives,' says Jackie Schneider, of Merton Parents for Better Food, a group which, as the name suggests, campaigns for better school meals. 'We were running around being very frenetic at the time. My worry was that we knew what we didn't want, but I wanted to know exactly what it was that we wanted to achieve. For example, it turned out that half of us wanted only organic food and half didn't. We needed to know what our stance was in order to talk to the authorities.' Schneider reports that it felt 'bizarre' going through that process 'at a time when nobody was taking us seriously'; however, it proved essential and provided the foundations for the campaign.

It is crucial to be clear that you know what your group is about. There is a phenomenon known as 'lowest common denominator campaigning'. If you can't agree on your aims and fail to get organisational sign-off, then everyone sticks to a half-hearted corporate line and campaign statements and demands sink to the 'lowest common denominator'.

For a campaign to have focus, you need to answer the following key questions:

- What is the nature of the problems you wish to solve?
- What are their causes and consequences?
- What is the range of possible solutions?

Examining the external factors

Remember that you do not exist in a vacuum. You need to think of your campaign in the wider context. The likelihood is that your own concerns, no matter how local, will have a resonance on a bigger national or even international stage. Parents were concerned about the quality of school meals years before Jamie Oliver brought the issue into the national consciousness with his 'School Dinners' campaign on Channel 4. New laws are passed on a national and European level which might further your cause (or hinder it). Elections, local and national, come and go and you should be alive to any way in which your campaign could be a critical issue. These are all opportunities for the campaigner. These issues are explored in greater detail in chapters 4 and 5.

The PEST analysis is a commonly used management tool to help you identify political, economic, social and technical factors which might influence your campaign. Try asking yourselves the following questions:

- **Political:** do you understand the political climate within which you operate? What are the policy-making structures that have an impact on your issue? Who are the political players?

- **Economic:** will economic conditions affect your campaign? Will the economic climate influence government spending relevant to your campaign? If you're working with companies, are economic issues likely to affect their involvement?

- **Social:** what social factors could influence your work? Is public opinion with you or against you? Are the media interested? Are there any celebrities supportive of your campaign?

- **Technical:** what are the technical/scientific influences on your campaign? Is scientific evidence stacked against you or for you? Can changing communications technology provide different routes for you to influence the decision-makers?

Examining internal factors

You need to understand whether you and your group have the capacity to take on the campaign, whether the issue is suitable, and whether time is well-spent. The following three questions will help you make such an evaluation:

1. Does your group have the legitimacy to run this campaign?
   - who do you speak for and have they been consulted?
   - do you speak with authority?

2. Are you prepared?
   - do you have the right management and decision-making systems in place?

3. Do you have the resources?
   - do you need to raise additional funds?

One way to help you pull together this information is to write down your internal and external analyses in the form of a SWOT (which stands for strengths, weaknesses, opportunities and threats) summary. So ask the following questions:

Strengths: what are the strengths of your campaign?

Weaknesses: what are its weaknesses?

Opportunities: what opportunities are there to further your campaign goals?

Threats: what threats are you aware of to undermine your campaign?

Developing the campaign strategy

Selecting the right solution

At this point you will have considered the problem, identified a range of potential solutions and developed an understanding of the internal and external context in which you are operating. In order to give your campaign real focus, you need to be able to answer the following two key questions:

1. Which solution offers the best potential impact for your group – in other words what will make a difference?

2. Which solution appears to be the most achievable (consider your SWOT summary)?

Unfortunately, it is unlikely that the solution with the greatest impact will also be the solution that is the most achievable. You and your supporters have to settle on an acceptable compromise.

Setting the campaign aim

Once you have identified the solution that you wish to achieve, it is now time to establish a clear campaign aim. What you need to do is formulate a mission statement (see the example on page 37). It should be easy to communicate to your supporters, the press, politicians and potential funders. In other words, it needs to be concise and clear. Ask yourself the following two questions:

1. Who needs to change for the desired solution to be achieved?

2. What needs to be different?

If there is more than one target, then you usually need more than one campaign.

Framing the campaign

'Framing' refers to the way in which issues are packaged and presented. The way your opponents (or those who simply are resistant to your message) frame your message, has an impact on the policy-makers whom you want to influence. Your challenge is to reframe your issue so people think about it in a different way and policy-makers perceive the issue in a way that best suits your interests.

There are various ways in which you can 'reframe' an issue:

- deliver in clear and engaging language;
- dramatise the concern;
- present a clear and credible solution; and
- outline the evidence of the problem, including a human story.

A striking example of effective 'reframing' has been Pro-Test, a pro-vivisection campaign (see chapter 6 for further details). This campaign managed to successfully redefine the terms of the animal research debate. Previously, the perceived moral high-ground had been the domain of anti-vivisectionists. Pro-Test is a group founded by a 16-year-old and led by students who successfully used new media (in particular, the social Internet networking sites) as a forum to create a new debate among the young (typically the demographic most vehemently opposed to animal testing).

Identifying routes of influence

Now you need to draw up how you will achieve your campaign aim. You need to identify the 'roots of influence'. In chapter 5, we suggest drawing an 'influence map' where you identify all the players who might have a bearing on the policy processes that relate to a particular issue. As a starting place, you should ask the following questions:

- Who is your campaign target (included in your aim)?
- How much influence do you and your allies have over the target?
- What and who influences the campaign target?
- What are the best ways for you to reach your target?

You need to familiarise yourself with political institutions and their decision-making processes. Again, chapter 5 further explores this territory.

Mission statement

Setting clear measurable objectives

You have identified your aim, so now is the time to identify the campaign objectives that guide you along the path towards that aim.

In the same way that your aim (or mission statement) should be clear and concise, so should your objectives (see example below). If possible, you should ensure your aim and objectives are prominent on your website and in any reports that you publish. An outsider should be able to read it and quickly have a clear understanding of what your group is about.

MISSION STATEMENT

MERTON PARENTS FOR BETTER FOOD IN SCHOOL

Aim

To ensure that school students are offered only good quality, healthy, appealing food, prepared and cooked from fresh ingredients on site in all our schools, served in a pleasant atmosphere.

Objectives

1. Merton Council takes on the process of a robust management of change to guarantee that the schools are provided and

---

continue to be provided with healthy fresh food.

2. A healthy balanced diet is offered at all schools.

3. Only good quality ingredients to be used in school meals

4. All cooking and food preparation to be done on site.

5. Eating lunch is a pleasant experience for children.

6. The school lunch becomes an integral part of the education offered by the school.

7. The Council sets up an effective system for monitoring school dinners, to ensure that the standards above are met and continue to be met.

8. To agree a target date by which all of the above will be achieved and clear, specific measurable milestones (no more than 6 months apart) on the path to these ultimate goals.

Your objectives are milestones of change which will help you focus and co-ordinate your campaigning effort to achieve maximum impact. The acronym SMART has come into common use in this context – objectives should be specific, measurable, achievable, realistic and time-based.

CASE STUDY: THE CONSUMER RIGHTS GROUP WHICH?

Adam Williams, media relations officer at Which?, talks about planning a campaign.

'Effective campaigns don't just happen – they take careful planning and execution. Passion and commitment when campaigning are important, but unless you are working to a plan, you could find yourself putting in a lot of time and energy without achieving results.

The first step is to set out your overall objective. What do you want to achieve?

Starting from your overall objective, work backwards looking at all of the smaller goals you need to achieve. It might help to organise a brainstorm with fellow campaigners to come up with ideas of how you are going to achieve your goals. Work out a rough timeline for your campaign and when you are likely to have peaks in activity. This will also help you to allocate resources and calculate budgets.

When working out the timing for each stage consider if there are any events on a local, regional or national level that you can use to promote your campaign to decision-makers or to the media. For example, if your campaign is about an issue that affects your local area, you might have more luck influencing your local MP or councillor with a major push in the run-up to an election or ahead of a major decision or announcement.

Co-ordinating the different aspects of your campaign so that they complement one another is also important to ensure optimum results for the effort you put in. For example, sending a petition to an MP is a good way of showing that your cause has support and publicising this through the media will help to highlight your cause and put pressure on the MP to act.

When embarking on a campaign it is vital that you have a strategy worked out to give you the best possible opportunity of achieving your goals. If you have a carefully planned strategy, then you can succeed with even the smallest resources.'

Developing work-plans

Once you have established your objectives, the next stage is to develop work-plans to see how the activity will be managed to achieve the objectives.

Work-planning involves:

- identifying the tasks that are necessary to deliver the objective;
- ensuring that the resources are available to be assigned to the tasks; and
- timetabling tasks.

There are many reasons to have a written work-plan – it makes it easier for people to be clear about what needs to be done, helps promote the understanding of your campaign within the group, enables resources to be allocated to tasks appropriately, as well as assisting in the monitoring process. However, those factors must be weighed against the fact that work-planning is time-consuming and it can quickly become out of date. It might well be worth seeing your campaign in terms of a six-month period.

Evaluation

This concluding section is a checklist of questions designed to test your plan:

Aim

- Does the campaign aim succinctly express what the campaign wants to achieve?
- Is it inspiring?
- Does it identify who needs to change and how they should change?
- Can you say with reasonable certainty that achieving this aim will have a positive impact on people's lives?
- Is there a commitment to keep campaigning until the goal is achieved?

Objectives

- Is it clear that the objectives you have identified are necessary in order to achieve the aim?
- Do they make clear the change that needs to happen?
- Are they measurable?
- Are they realistic given the resources available?
- Are systems in place to monitor and evaluate progress?

Outputs

- Is it clear that the activities you want to organise will contribute to the achievement of these outputs?

- Do they describe together a set of achievements that are needed to attain the outcomes you have identified?

- Is there a set of practical actions to achieve each output?

- Are systems in place to ensure efficient use of resources?

Activities

- Are the major activities listed?

- Is the list manageable?

- Do they reflect main actions required to achieve the outputs?

- Are resources identified that will help you deliver these activities?

- Are these resources sufficient?

It is important to keep revisiting this approach in checking the assumptions behind, and the progress of, the campaign throughout its duration.

This structured approach to planning and managing your campaign can and should be applied in a mini-form for particular tasks, such as fundraising or preparing for publicity. Good preparation is a vital ingredient for success. Planning is simply an effective way of preparing properly for the task.

CHAPTER 3

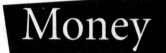

Money

> 'We didn't ask for people's money. We asked for their time and energy. To be honest, there's nothing that we would have done differently or better if we had the money at the start.'
>
> Jackie Schneider, of Merton Parents for Better Food and winner of the Sheila McKechnie Foundation's consumer action award 2006

The key message regarding money is – don't let a lack of it stand in your way. Small-scale local campaign groups and pressure groups, almost always, operate on a shoestring. Local start-up groups in the *People Power* questionnaire claimed that a lack of resources was the most difficult barrier in the early days of their campaigns. However, it was a handicap that rarely appeared to halt the progress of successful campaigns. Local grass roots initiatives are powered by the enthusiasm of the supporters rather than ready cash.

Depending on how many supporters you have and their energies, you can go a long way on very little. You can host your first meeting at the local church hall for nothing more than the cost of refreshments if your local vicar is sympathetic to the cause. You can print 1,500 flyers for £500 (design and order online for next day delivery). There is also the zero-budget option. The first meeting takes place in your local pub, everyone gets a round in, and flyers are designed and printed by you and your friends on your home PC, etc.

One of the most energising aspects about community-based organisations comes from a group of like-minded people relying on their own resourcefulness. In the age of the Internet, effective campaigns can be run from a bedroom at little or no cost. The Ban Foie Gras campaign and Pro-Test are two such examples considered at greater length in chapter 6. But also be prepared to be surprised – enthusiastic supporters are often very happy to put their hands in their pockets (and some are more than happy to sign fairly hefty cheques). You need to think of what you can do if your group is the lucky recipient of some money.

Some campaigners who responded to the questionnaire were less than convinced, even suspicious, about fundraising, seeing it as a distraction from the main point of a group. 'Having money just makes things more complicated,' comments Jackie Schneider. 'We've managed to make really big changes in terms of the thinking behind school dinner hour and the schools themselves have made huge changes with very small funds because they have seen it as a priority. With that in mind, I see it as laughable that a grass roots campaigning organisation could complain that they cannot get off the ground because of a lack of funds. If people feel passionately and want to spend time on something, then they will.'

Others viewed external financial support as representing an unacceptable loss of independence. 'We needed the support of a professional office which our [lack of] finances precluded,' says Suzanne Walker, of the Uttlesford district group of the Campaign to Protect Rural England. 'But self-funding is necessary to maintain independence from outside influence.' She reckons that the group ran on about £30 a week, with main costs being stationery and travel.

You need to plan ahead. There are a number of very good reasons for thinking about how your group will organise itself in terms of its finances. If you have a whip-round to get started, who holds the £150? Do you put it in a tin? Do you, as treasurer, put it in your own bank account? (Not a great idea.) Do you open a group bank account? (Yes.) For what reason are you holding the money? You might think a trip to lobby MPs is useful, others might not. Be clear. On a very practical level, these issues can be a diverting headache but, on top of that, there are legal implications which need to be considered. Keep it simple.

Be mindful that as your group grows, more sophisticated fundraising tactics might be contemplated; then you need to be more alert that there will be practical as well as legal and tax implications.

'We've spotted a real trend with very wealthy people – the people who live on their 40-acre estates on the outskirts of the village – who are really concerned about climate change. They want to do their bit in the way they know how,' reports one campaigner in the Stop Bristol Airport Expansion coalition. Their group received £40,000 in one go from one such supporter. The money, she explains, is used according to need. In other words, it isn't just a £40,000 one-off sum; but a commitment to spend that sum for research, promotional materials and paying for noise impact reports.

> **CHAPTER OVERVIEW:**
>
> - Handling money
> - Raising money – general principles
> - Raising money – techniques

Model Financial Forecast

	Apr £	May £	Jun £	Jul £	Aug £	Sep £	Oct £	Nov £	Dec £	Jan £	Feb £	Mar £	TOTAL £
RECEIPTS													
Donations from individuals	10	10	10	10	10	10	10	10	10	10	10	10	120
Bank interest	-	-	1	-	-	2	-	15	15	-	-	3	21
Donations from local businesses	50	-	250	-	-	-	40	15	-	-	-	-	355
Proceeds from car boot sale	-	-	-	-	-	197	-	-	-	-	-	-	197
Donation from ABC PLC	-	-	1,000	-	-	-	-	-	-	-	-	-	1,000
Grant from XYZ charity	-	-	-	-	-	-	-	-	2,500	-	-	-	2,500
etc													
TOTAL RECEIPTS	**60**	**10**	**1,261**	**10**	**10**	**209**	**50**	**25**	**2,525**	**10**	**10**	**13**	**4,193**
EXPENSES													
Bank charges	5	5	5	5	5	5	5	5	5	5	5	5	60
Travel costs to Parliament	-	-	-	60	-	-	-	-	-	-	-	115	175
Leaflet costs	-	-	875	-	-	-	-	-	875	-	-	-	1,750
Legal advice	-	-	-	-	-	-	-	-	500	-	-	-	500
Meeting costs	13	-	-	14	-	-	13	-	-	13	-	27	80
Postage	-	1	10	200	-	-	-	-	-	400	-	-	611
Website costs	-	-	-	-	-	200	-	-	-	-	-	300	500
Advertising	40	-	-	-	-	-	100	-	100	-	-	100	340
etc													
TOTAL PAYMENTS	**58**	**6**	**890**	**279**	**5**	**205**	**118**	**5**	**1,480**	**418**	**5**	**547**	**4,016**
TOTAL RECEIPTS LESS PAYMENTS	2	4	371	-269	5	4	-68	20	1,045	-408	5	-534	177
OPENING BANK BALANCE	-	2	6	377	108	113	117	49	69	1,114	706	711	-
CLOSING BANK BALANCE	2	6	377	108	113	117	49	69	1,114	706	711	177	177

Handling money

Budget

You need to keep control of your finances. Campaigns are organic and unpredictable, but there is much to be gained from writing a clear budget, comparing receipts with expenses and projecting expenditure over the next 12 months. See model financial forecast on the opposite page.

Trigger points

Local campaign groups tend to be informal without any corporate structure (often unincorporated associations), as discussed in chapter 1. If you are a small local group, then keep things informal. In the following section, we have identified the following four major financial 'trigger points' where you might want to take professional advice.

1. **Are you handling money?** The starting point should be, if you are holding money then at the very least you need to consider having a governing document, or a constitution. This is dealt with in chapter 1, but it has a special significance in relation to handling money and raising funds. At the very least, adopting a formal agreement will impose a degree of discipline on your thinking and could pre-empt any potential wranglings over money. It might also limit (to a degree) personal liability, as well as deal specifically with how money will be held, how funds can be accessed and by whom, as well as providing for what happens when your group's objectives are achieved but funds are left over. In addition when you open a group bank account (a very good idea) then the bank will expect such a document.

2. **Can you do everything you need to do?** If you are a more informal group or unincorporated association, then you have no legal identity beyond that of you and your fellow supporters. This means that your group, for example, cannot borrow

money or enter into a contract to rent premises. Such arrangements will have to be done in your individual names. Is that what you want?

3. **Does your group have an income of over £5,000?** If you want to register as a charity, you have to have an income in excess of £5,000. If you want to raise money to support a good cause, do you have to register as a charity? No. It is not necessary to be a charity in order to raise funds; however, only charities can raise money using the word 'charity' or 'charitable'.

4. **Do you want to limit your liability?** One of the risks of being an unincorporated association is that anything you do could potentially trigger the personal liability of your members. The benefit of running your campaign through, for example, a limited company is that it is the company that forms contracts with third parties and takes on any liabilities, not you personally. If your group is an unincorporated association, you and your management committee will have unlimited personal liability and so, for example, you could face a legal action if one of your more enthusiastic members libelled the owner of the local incinerator you have been campaigning to close down (see chapter 8). The risks of any personal liability may well be low enough not to require your campaign to exist as a company, but if your group is developing a critical mass then it makes sense to consider becoming a company limited by guarantee (see chapter 1). Most national campaign groups are limited companies as opposed to unincorporated associations. With a limited company the corporate entity employs staff, owns property, holds bank accounts, and enters into contracts in its own name and is liable for debts and legal actions.

As discussed in chapter 1, your constitution should clearly lay down how money should be handled by your group. Just as in any relationship, it is often disputes over the finances that create the greatest friction in community groups. No matter how philanthropic you and your supporters' motives are, do not be naïve. Bear in mind that one in 20 'not-for-profit' groups have experienced frauds of over £10,000 in the last three years (Baker Tilly's *Voluntary*

Sector Governance Survey 2007). Therefore, it makes sense to have a group bank account. Most high street banks will open up an account for an unincorporated association if you have a constitution (sometimes they call it a 'community account'). According to the HSBC, any 'clubs, societies or associations' wishing to open such an account are required to provide the bank with a copy of 'their constitution or rules', plus you will have to identify and verify the addresses of all signatories to new accounts. For security purposes, you are required to have at least two signatories. It's a good idea to have three or four signatories, so that if people are on holiday cheques can still be signed.

Your constitution should lay out the treasurer's responsibility. Typically, a treasurer might be allowed to approve any individual items of expenditure up to, say, £50 as specified in the constitution. Beyond that sum, then the treasurer plus one other person would be expected to approve any expenditure.

TOP TIPS

- Keep a written set of finance procedures.

- Make sure your management committee is aware of their responsibilities and that your treasurer has the required financial know-how and business background – additional training may be needed.

- Set up a proper financial system from the beginning. Try to set aside some time each week to deal with receipts and paperwork. This way they won't get lost.

- Decisions about expenditure should only be made by people authorised to do so.

- Ensure that the treasurer makes regular financial reports to the committee and that bank statements are regularly reconciled.

- Work within an agreed budget. This will allow expenditure to be monitored and ensure that your costs do not exceed your limits.

- Have two people who are responsible for handling and

recording money. For example:

- always have two signatories to sign cheques;

- open post in the presence of two people;

- have two people take money to the bank; and

- never sign blank cheques!

- Split up duties. Divide your financial processes into tasks and allocate each to a different person. People can check each other's tasks before carrying out their own. This helps to avoid mistakes and makes fraud difficult to go undetected.

- Receipts and invoices should be obtained for all payments. Ensure cash collections and donations are paid into your group's bank account.

- Your organisation's money should always be separate from personal money.

- Don't allow a bank account to remain dormant.

- Never keep more cash on the premises than is necessary.

- Petty cash – access should be restricted and the petty cash book should be written up and balanced regularly. Cash in hand should be accounted for.

Source: Community Links, Bromley

Tax

If your group is registered as a charity, then you will be exempt from a number of taxes (see later). But if you are not yet registered as a charity then you will not be entitled to exemptions unless you have gained official exemption from HM Revenue & Customs. Bear in mind that you are not liable for tax on donations (this includes gifts and subscriptions). However, any profits from trading (e.g. running a cake stall, selling t-shirts, etc) or fundraising, including bank interest, will be liable to Corporation Tax. The calculation of trading profits in a charity is subject to an allowance of £5,000 per annum before Corporation Tax becomes payable. This allowance can also be increased in certain circumstances dependent on the income of the charity. An exception is profits from occasional fundraising events (like a fete, dinner-dance, jumble sale, etc) which are not taxable. If you think that you might be liable to pay tax on profits you are making, then contact your local tax office.

If your income from business supplies (trading or services for which you charge, not donations) exceeds the VAT threshold (in the year 2006/07 it was £61,000), then you may have to register for VAT and charge VAT on goods and services provided. If you think you will reach that threshold, then you need to contact HM Revenue & Customs. Contrary to popular belief, registered charities do not have a blanket exemption from VAT but are exempt from certain payments. Otherwise you will be treated just as any other organisation.

Raising money – general principles

Most of the groups who responded to our questionnaire did engage in fundraising activities – but not all. Usually they relied on the generosity of their membership, through donations or membership subscription schemes.

Within a small-scale campaign, everyone in the group is a potential fundraiser. They should all have a clear understanding of the group's aims and objectives (see chapter 2) so that they can communicate that with potential donors.

Developing a fundraising strategy

The Institute of Fundraising recommends the following considerations:

- **What are your group's aims and objectives?** Your fundraising strategy should be based on this – see chapter 1.

- **What are the internal and external influences that might affect your group?** We have already discussed the usefulness of conducting a SWOT and PEST analysis – again see chapter 2. For a SWOT analysis (standing for strengths, weaknesses, opportunities and threats), there will be strengths and weaknesses in your group; for example, you may have the strength of 200 members but a weakness in having no dedicated fundraiser. Opportunities and threats usually come from outside, and so, for example, an opportunity might be the development of a new fundraising technique and a threat might be a larger organisation starting to fundraise among your own members.

- **What are your fundraising aims?** Examples of a fundraising aim might be to commission research.

- **What are your income sources?** There are four main funding partners: trusts and foundations, companies, individuals, and community groups (see next section).

- **What fundraising methods will help you achieve your aims?** The techniques you choose will be influenced by your SWOT analysis, the nature of the prospective funding, and the length of time you have to raise funds (e.g. if there is a three-month deadline on a consultation).

- **What are your resources and budget?** You need to arrive at a firm estimate of these.

The fundraising cycle

Fundraisers use a planning tool called 'the fundraising cycle' to help them monitor and develop activities. It helps ensure a group's fundraising activities benefit donors and beneficiaries to their utmost. Fundraisers use many different techniques to communicate with donors and potential donors, such as events, direct mail, competitions and lotteries.

The case for support: a statement that explains why a donor should give to the charity. It must contain enough information to

THE FUNDRAISING CYCLE (developed by Redmond Mullin)

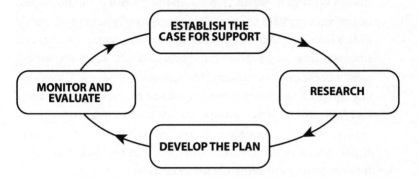

enable a donor to make an informed decision to give to your cause. This could be as brief as a simple side of A4 (but for a major application, the case for support may contain thousands of words, pictures and plans).

The statement needs to be concise, coherent, urgent and motivating, and communicate:

- all about the organisation and its activities (possibly include your mission statement);

- the level of need and why it is urgent (use case studies of real people or activities where possible and use facts and figures);

- the specific objectives of the appeal;

- your group's history and recent successes to illustrate why you are the most suitable organisation to make a difference;

- what would happen if you did not run this appeal or the appeal failed;

- how much money an appeal is trying to raise and over what period of time (stress the urgency and break down total sums needed into smaller amounts to form a 'shopping list' for donors);

- how will each donation make a difference (show how a potential gift will translate into a tangible benefit); and

- who else is involved (mention any other local groups).

Research: the second stage of the cycle is essential to inform the group about which donors might respond to the appeal outlined in the case for support. Research will help you identify individuals, companies or trusts most likely to respond and so research might involve conducting Web searches, using reference books, subscribing to specialist research databases, searching through your existing database, testing marketing materials on a small group, asking other organisations for advice or help, investigating possible trusts that might have suitable grants, and researching local businesses. For more information about research, see chapter 7.

Planning: the third step is to plan and implement fundraising activities, taking into account relevant internal and external factors which may influence a success. Plan activities to ensure that they are adequately resourced, cost-effective and efficient, and help reduce and manage any risks.

Monitoring and evaluation: finally, during and after the fundraising activity it is important to monitor and evaluate the successes and failures of the activity (see chapter 9). This tells you how to make the activity bigger and better the next time and what lessons to learn if it has not been as successful as you would have liked.

The fundraising cycle then begins again, building on successes, minimising failures, developing relationships with donors and identifying new fundraising opportunities.

IS IT WORTH IT?

The Institute of Fundraising suggests a simple formula:

Funds raised ÷ total cost of activity = cost-effectiveness.

Remember to include all costs when calculating the total cost of activities. Cost-effectiveness can be expressed as a ratio, either as a percentage or as a multiplier – for example, 25% or 4:1. So, for example:

- for every £4 raised, £1 (or 25%) has been spent to raise it;

> - for every £1 spent on fundraising, £4 been generated as income.
>
> This is often called the 'return on investment', or the 'ROI' of an activity; for example, the Institute of Fundraising reckons as a rule of thumb applications to trusts and foundations (see later) for financial support can have a return of £9 for each £1 spent on raising them; whereas direct marketing in the early stages of recruiting donors may only have a 1:1, or lower return. You need to establish what ROI you are comfortable with.

Fundraisers

Anyone in your group who has the right skills can be a suitable candidate. A good fundraiser has the following attributes:

- communication skills;
- planning and organisational ability;
- judgment, tact and diplomacy;
- empathy with the cause;
- understanding of finance and budgeting; and
- creativity.

While the larger groups will be able to employ dedicated fundraisers (or consultants), smaller community-based outfits will not. Volunteers can be a great asset to your group. Further information on working with volunteers is available at www.volunteering england.org.uk. If you do consider using consultants or professional fundraisers, you can agree set fees for specific pieces of work or payment for hours worked. The Institute of Fundraising does not recommend commission-based payments alone where payment is determined by calculating a percentage of the total money that is raised. Commission runs the risk that donors may be pressurised into giving or that fundraisers may receive inappropriate remuneration.

For more information, see www.institute-of-fundraising.org.uk.

Basic principles

A good starting point is the Institute of Fundraising's Code of Fundraising Practice available on the Institute's website. The most important point is always to ensure that any fundraising literature is absolutely clear about the activities of your group and the purpose of the fundraising activity.

In particular, if you're choosing to fundraise for a particular cause, then any money raised must be used for that cause. The income raised must be put into a 'restricted' fund and used only for that purpose. You need to consider the eventuality that more money will be raised than is needed and make sure that any fundraising materials state how such funds will be used.

Charities should state that they are a registered charity. The Charity Commission has powers to investigate the activities of charities. A scheme for self-regulation of fundraising has been set up (see the Fundraising Standards Board, www.frsb.org.uk).

You also need to think about data protection issues. If you're going to hold personal information, such as names, addresses and telephone numbers of donors on your database, you might need to register with the Information Commissioner's Office. For further information (including a handy online self-assessment form which will determine whether you need to register), see www.ico.gov.uk.

If your group approaches donors or potential donors whether by direct mail, email or phone, you must give the donor the opportunity to opt out, or choose not to hear from you again.

For more information, see www.institute-of-fundraising.org.uk

DATA PROTECTION: THE BASICS

The Data Protection Act 1998 gives individuals the right to know what information is held about them and provides a framework to ensure that personal information is handled properly. The Act works in two ways. Firstly, it states that anyone who processes personal information must comply with eight principles, which make sure that personal information is:

1. fairly and lawfully processed;

2. processed for limited purposes;

3. adequate, relevant and not excessive;

4. accurate and up-to-date;

5. not kept for longer than is necessary;

6. processed in line with your rights;

7. secure; and

8. not transferred to other countries without adequate protection.

The second area covered by the Act provides individuals with important rights, including the right to find out what personal information is held on computer and most paper records.

For more information about data protection, see the Information Commissioner's Office at www.ico.gov.uk.

People may register their details on a variety of preference services such as the Mailing Preference Service (www.mpsonline.org.uk) and the Telephone Preference Service (www.tpsonline.org.uk). These services log that an individual does not want to receive communications they have not requested. Groups should check any list of individuals against the preference services.

TOP TIPS

• If you are a registered charity, always state that you are registered with the Charity Commission.

• Make it clear what the donors' money will be used for.

• Comply with data protection.

• Ask donors how they would like to be communicated with – and don't forget to thank them.

Raising money – techniques

Membership subscriptions

The enthusiastic backing of your own supporters will be one of your most valuable sources of funds. If you increase your membership base, then you may correspondingly increase income through subscription drives or appeals for donations. Unlike fundraising events (see later), membership income can provide a more reliable and steady flow of campaign funds. It is one of the most common ways of funding campaign groups; for example, Demand Group, which has been calling for a cap on flights into Nottingham East Midlands Airport, has a minimum subscription for its 1,400 members of a one-off £5, and Surfers Against Sewage has yearly membership fees starting at £12 for the unemployed, £18 for individuals and £24 for a family.

Money can come in from direct debits or standing orders. Include a direct debit form in your newsletter or ask prospective members over the phone if they would be willing to give regularly.

For any start-up group, you might want to consider a membership drive. You should consider making as many people as possible aware of the new group and what it stands for. There are a number of cheap and easy ways to promote your group; for example, a media campaign with mailshots to households in the area, or a leaflet to send out with mailings from like-minded groups. You could also consider putting notices up in community centres to advertise for new members.

How high should subscriptions be set? Membership subscriptions can range from £5 to £100 a year, depending on the generosity of your backers. They need to be set at a level that you think your members, or potential members, might regard as acceptable but at the same time sufficient to ensure that enough members will be prepared to pay. Don't aim too low either, for fear of scaring off would-be members – at the very least, you need to budget carefully to ensure that you cover the costs of the membership drive. Compare your proposed subscription rates with those of similar organisations.

Also consider a discounted rate for young people, students and the unemployed. You should always allow the opportunity for potential donors to make a one-off donation – some people do not like the commitment of a direct debit arrangement.

Individual donors

Individuals are hugely supportive of good causes – the public donated over £8 billion to charity in 2005. Almost two-thirds of the population (60%) claim to have given to charity in the last month. Most donations come from individuals giving one-off cash gifts, but a growing number (10 million donors) give regularly via monthly direct debit schemes.

TOP TIPS

- Ask donors if they would consider a direct debit.
- Keep donors updated on your work, possibly through a regular newsletter.
- At a later date, ask donors if they would be willing to increase their donation.
- Respect the wishes of donors who ask not to be contacted again.
- Ask donors if they wish to 'gift aid' (see below) their donations.

What is the best way to ask donors for a donation? There are many different ways of asking individuals to make gifts. Use the case for support on page 53 to underpin your fundraising appeal. Remember to thank donors for their donations and to tell them what their gift has enabled your group to do. Consider the following methods:

- **Face-to-face fundraising**
  Collecting money from passers-by or knocking on doors is a traditional method of fundraising. It is a good way to raise the profile of your group within your community as well as raising

one-off donations from people's loose change. Your supporters can collect money and hand out group stickers as a 'thank you'. Another option is to ask shops to place sealed collecting tins on their counters. Ask permission from the shop manager first and once a month or so return to collect it. Another practice is to ask individuals to sign up to give a regular donation via direct debit.

Public collections are regulated under the Charities Act 1992. You will need a permit from your local authority if you are organising a street or a house-to-house collection. It applies not only to charities but to any appeal for 'charitable, benevolent or philanthropic purposes'. Permits normally have to be applied for at least one month before you want to collect. To do without the correct permit or authority could well be a criminal offence. To be sure, check with your local council about obtaining a permit. If the collection is not made in a public place or by house-to-house visits, no permit is needed. So you do not need one if you are holding a public meeting, at an event where you need a ticket, in a shop or a theatre, or if you are collecting via unmanned collection boxes. By way of example, if you are raising money in a shopping centre, you need a permit.

You will be up against competition from the more professional national charities, and remember that the public often suffer from compassion fatigue. Not everyone wants to be accosted on the streets by fundraisers.

TOP TIPS

- Contact the local authority well in advance to obtain a permit or licence.

- Equip volunteers with sealed and labelled collecting tins and with personal identification badges.

- Open and count money raised in the presence of at least two individuals.

- Read *Your Right to Peaceful Protest – A guide* (see Appendix 6) for further guidance on collecting money.

- **Direct mail**

  Approach your donors by hand-delivered flyers, emails, newsletters or mailshots. Many groups build a database of 'warm donors' (donors who have already expressed an interest in your group and have already donated) whom they approach three or four times a year asking for donations.

- **Telephone fundraising**

  This allows donors to have direct conversations with representatives. Also consider using SMS (the donor texts a message 'DONATE' to a telephone number included in an advert, the donor receives a 'thank you' message back, and your group receives a proportion of the cost of each text).

- **Press and media**

  Use your local newspaper or radio station to cover a fundraising event, or pitch a story about your group's activities to them. Local newspapers often like 'good news' stories.

  One option is to ask a local radio or television station to run a feature on the work of your group. Many have a regular appeal slot which can be booked; for example, Radio 4's *The Week's Good Cause*.

- **Internet**

  If you intend to collect donations through your site, it needs to be secure.

How much should you ask for? It is a good idea to offer examples of possible amounts, particularly as donors are not always sure how much might be appropriate. Try a shopping list of items that they might wish to 'buy' – for example, '£10 would cover the cost of 100 flyers' or '£250 would cover the cost of commissioning research into pollution levels around the proposed incinerator'. If someone has been prepared to pay £5 for the previous 12 months, consider asking for £8 or £10 next year.

Also consider the occasion. Larger sums might be donated at a fundraising dinner party than at a cash collection on the street.

CASE STUDY: DEMAND GROUP

'Knock on the doors of wealthy people, but don't exclude others, because you will need the ground floor support as well,' advises Steve Charlish, who founded the Demand Group, currently battling for a cap on flights into Nottingham East Midlands Airport. He started the group from scratch following concerns about the expansion of the airport, which he was alerted to through his job as a commercial pilot. 'I made a beeline for the stately homes and biggest houses, because they were the people who have the influence and the money,' he says.

The first person he approached gave him a cheque for £1,000, which kick-started the campaign. More than 1,000 people turned up for that first meeting. The group has a minimum subscription for its 1,400 members of £5. The campaign is expensive to run – its phone bill for the first 12 months was in the region of £1,500, stationery costs for newsletters to 100,000 houses came to £3,000, and a noise survey by an independent consultant cost £5,000.

Gift aid

It is a form of tax relief that's only available to charities. HM Revenue & Customs treats donations as if the donor has already deducted basic rate tax. The charity can then reclaim this tax to increase the value of a donation. This means that any donation from an individual could be worth around 25% more to the charity.

There are a number of ways that the government encourages individuals and groups to give to charities, such as if an individual leaves a legacy to a charity, then that donation will be exempt from Inheritance Tax. If an employee gives to charity directly from their employer's payroll, they automatically receive tax relief on their donation as well as providing a charity with regular and reliable income. In addition, if an individual donates their land or shares to a charity, then the donation will be exempt from Capital Gains Tax and the individual will also receive Income Tax relief and taxpayers who fill in self-assessment returns can choose to donate any tax rebate they may be owed to a charity.

Events

From hosting a dinner dance at a local restaurant to organising a sponsored walk, events are a popular way of raising funds – £51 million was raised through fundraising events by the top 500 charities in 2004. 'The most effective events are the big headline ones which take a lot of organising and hours of your time, but bring in lots of funds at once,' reckons Sharon Makinson, the campaign secretary of the Denholme Residents' Action Group, set up to fight a planning application to use a local quarry for a landfill site (see chapter 1). Her experience is that the fundraising 'in dribs and drabs', such as jumble sales, brought in 'little return for the effort and are exhausting'. 'Our biggest successes were a sponsored Millennium Walk in West Yorkshire,' she says. 'We were the first group to walk this new right of way, which covered over 42 miles in two days. We also organised two rock concerts in the local hotel and a dog show, which had various silly classes of dogs, bouncy castles and other shows. A local enthusiast also gave a sheep herding demonstration, but used ducks instead of sheep. We also put out a begging bowl for public meetings. At our first meeting we collected just over £250. However, at our most successful public meeting we collected over £3,000 in one go. It was all a real measure of the village support for our campaign.'

Dinners and entertainment

Consider holding a disco, dinner dance, garden fete, cheese and wine party or pub quiz. Keep costs to a minimum. Do you know any local dignitaries or celebrities who might deliver an after-dinner speech for free? Could a local company donate a prize for the raffle?

> **TOP TIPS**
> * Check whether an entertainment licence is required by contacting the local authority.
> * Ensure volunteers and staff attending the event are fully briefed.
> * Ensure the venue complies with health and safety regulations and is accessible to all.

Local schools and youth groups

Many local schools and youth groups might want to help by organising an event to support your charity. You need to seek permission from the head teacher, bear in mind the age and capability of young people when designing fundraising activities, try to ensure that your proposals fit in with the school curriculum, and ensure activities are safe and legal.

Clubs and associations

It might be appropriate to contact community groups like your local Rotary Club. You might even find that they express an interest in fundraising in aid of your organisation.

Competitions, raffles and lotteries

Events that are synonymous with community groups are organising a tombola or the selling of raffle tickets. There is a legal framework covering the running of any 'lottery', which includes raffles, tombolas, prize draws, sweepstakes through to 'Name that Teddy' draws.

All lotteries are illegal unless they are exempt or authorised by the Lotteries and Amusements Act 1976. Before you organise a fundraising draw, make sure it is:

* not deemed to be a lottery; or
* qualifies as an 'exempted entertainment' lottery (see below).

An exempted entertainment is a bazaar, sale of work, fete, dinner, dance, sporting or athletic event under the 1976 Act.

There are three types of lottery under current law:

1. **Small lottery.** Tickets don't have to be specially printed and there is no limit on sale price but no more than £250 should be spent on purchasing prizes. Cash prizes are not allowed (although vouchers are). 'Small lotteries' must be run as part of another event, for example, a pub quiz or a dinner, and you can only sell tickets to people attending.

2. **Private lottery.** Can only be offered to people who live or work at the same premises or who belong to the same membership organisation. Proceeds must be split between prizes and the membership organisation. Tickets can be printed but a sweepstake is also allowed.

3. **Society lottery.** To sell tickets to the general public, groups need to run a 'society lottery'. Your local authority or the Gambling Commission, depending on the size of the lottery, regulates such events. If sales of tickets exceed £20,000 for a single lottery or £250,000 in one calendar year, then you must register with the Gambling Commission, otherwise contact the licensing officer at your local authority. The maximum permitted price of a ticket is £2 and should not be bought or sold by young people (i.e. under 16 years old).

    The Gambling Act 2005 changed the rules of society lotteries in September 2007 and at the time of going to press the regime has yet to be finalised. Check the current position with the Gambling Commission (www.gamblingcommission.gov.uk).

The benefits of running a lottery

-   Prizes can be donated.
-   Funds raised by small and private lotteries are unrestricted.
-   Income from private and small lotteries are exempt from tax.

You might consider having a competition or a free prize draw if the lottery rules are problematic.

- **Competition.** There must be sufficient skill involved in the competition so that it does not inadvertently become an illegal lottery. Unfortunately, there is no definition of what constitutes 'sufficient skill'. Consider including a question about the activities of the charity which requires a little research or a tie-breaker. Make sure that the rules of entry are clear and terms and any conditions are included in the offer. Marketing, advertising and rules of entry should comply with the Advertising Standards Authority's non-broadcast code of advertising practice. Tickets will be subject to VAT unless they are sold during an exempt event (see above).

- **Free prize draw.** This enables you to offer supporters a prize and engage the public in a game of chance. It is not a lottery. Your promotional material should state that no donation is necessary. You must not insist on a minimum donation, though 'suggested donation' may be acceptable.

Raising money from businesses

Companies are increasingly likely to contribute to their local community and many will have corporate social responsibility programmes. However, you may find that the interests of your group are diametrically opposed to business. The private sector is also the least generous when it comes to support for voluntary groups. The NCVO in a 2004 report found only 5% of the total voluntary income came from this sector. According to research, 45% of fundraising costs were spent on companies which delivered only 8% of the total income.

Personal contacts are important; think of links between your group and the work of the company you are targeting. Sending unsolicited letters is unlikely to meet with a great response. Remember that some companies have their own grant-making trusts – for example, the Lloyds TSB Foundation. Business in the Community is an organisation which was set up to strengthen the links between businesses and their local community. It may be able to find volunteers who have specific skills which could help your organisation. Companies could also fundraise for you.

There is an obvious difference between donations and sponsorship:

- A donation is given without any expectation of anything in return. The donor may be able to donate equipment such as computers, or they may be able to donate staff time to help you with specific projects.

- Sponsorship is a two-way agreement between your group and the company. Are there any local businesses which can provide money or gifts in kind? A local businessman might be able to support a local event by having his name on campaign literature.

You might also consider 'cause-related marketing': this is where a local restaurant may donate 5% from every bill, or a hairdresser donates £1 from every haircut to the group. Ensure that there is a contract between you and the business setting out the terms and conditions in full (the Institute of Fundraising has its own model contract). Make sure that the amount you receive from the sale of a product or service is stated clearly in any advertising or printed material. Think about what the business does and how it might conflict with the causes and values of your group.

TOP TIPS

- Potential businesses might be willing to sponsor an event, newsletter or other activity.
- Agree the scope of the sponsorship.
- Invite employees along to the event and remember to thank them afterwards.
- Charge businesses separately for the use of their logo.
- Promote the partnership to the local media.

Trusts, foundations and other sources

There are in the region of 8,800 trusts and foundations in the UK, ranging from the Big Lottery Fund to regional funders such as the Lloyds TSB Foundations and Community Foundations. It is thought that 90% of money comes from the top 300 grant-making trusts.

UK trusts and foundations give about £2.7 billion in grants each year. Trust funding represents about 10% of the voluntary sector's income – and is similar in total to central government spending.

Trusts and foundations give grants to groups where their projects or activities match funding objectives. Some trusts are limited by their charitable powers and so can only give to groups supporting particular issues relating to, for example, children or women.

According to the umbrella group the Association of Charitable Foundations, trusts and foundations like to fund 'what government does not fund'. In particular, they are interested in:

- new methods of tackling problems;
- disadvantaged and minority groups who have trouble using ordinary services, or who have inadequate access to services;
- responses to new or newly discovered needs and problems;
- work which is hard to finance through conventional fundraising;
- one-off purchases or projects;
- short- and medium-term work which is likely to bring a long-term benefit and/or to attract long-term funding from elsewhere.

Larger trusts such as the Esmée Fairbairn Foundation have their own criteria and methods for making applications. They have staff employed to assess candidates for funding. Other trusts are managed by a group of volunteer trustees who get together once or twice a year to make decisions. Do your research before making an application.

Trusts support organisations in a number of ways. They could offer project funding over a number of years; capital funding towards, for example, equipment; or they might support start-up funding to enable you to try out a new project. Increasingly trusts are backing revenue and salary costs or offering loans or matched funding for projects. Trusts tend to prefer a proposal where they can see their support will make a tangible difference. To identify potential trusts and foundations, check out www.trustfunding.org.uk. The Association of Charitable Foundations has links from its website to individual trust websites as well as hints and tips on making applications (www.acf.org.uk).

CASE STUDY: XTRAORDINARY PEOPLE

Xtraordinary People was set up by Kate Griggs in 2004 to raise awareness and funding to support dyslexia training in schools. The group has just been given a £900,000 pump-priming fund from the government over two years which they have to match.

Kate sees this as a measure of the success of the campaign: 'If the government puts nearly £1 million into a project, it means that they genuinely think what you are saying is right,' she says. However, she adds that the group has not, up until this point, needed money: 'In our infancy the campaign didn't cost anything. We did everything for nothing. The website didn't cost anything, the PR didn't cost us anything, and I didn't even get my expenses back.' She even stood against the education minister, Ruth Kelly, in the 2005 general election and met those considerable costs out of her own pocket.

'Between now and the next 18 months we have to raise the best part of £1 million – and that is very daunting,' Kate says. 'Our group has gone from being a personal campaign to where we have to prove ourselves to the government and use its money to demonstrate unequivocally what should be happening in schools. It makes it very pressurised.'

CHAPTER 4

The message

> 'When the *Evening Standard* rang up the first time I was petrified. We thought that they would turn on us and see us all as middle class. But after I spoke to the press a few times I realised that the world wouldn't end and soon I came to see them as a friend.'
>
> Jackie Schneider of Merton Parents for Better Food

This chapter considers the main ways that campaigners can use to ensure that their voice is heard in the press. People who have had few dealings with the media are understandably nervous about how they will be treated by journalists. If that's the case, you need to overcome your fears. A sympathetic journalist is a vital ally. A high-profile presence in the press will help you recruit new supporters, put pressure on local and national decision-makers and force them to respond to your demands. The media can help you to publicise a specific event or part of your campaign, and above all raise the profile of the objective you are trying to achieve. But remember, winning good press isn't an end in itself.

Behind successful campaigns there is a strong communications strategy. Careful planning at the outset will give all your external communications a clear, concise and consistent message. Campaigns take on a life of their own and it's all too easy to lose sight of your objectives.

Basic principles that apply to the campaign as a whole can also be applied to each individual activity you choose to do. For example, if you decide to arrange a public meeting you need to think about your objectives, who you are addressing, when and where it will be, and who in your group will be responsible. If you are considering sending out a press release – what are your objectives? What audience are you addressing? When is the release to be sent out for maximum effect? Who in the group is responsible? A clear and strategic approach to all your external communications shows that you and your campaign should be taken seriously.

CHAPTER OVERVIEW:

- Working with the media
- Other campaigning techniques
- Public meetings

Working with the media

The way that you present your message can be every bit as important as what you actually say when it comes to delivering your message effectively. The clarity and quality of your letter writing, press releases and the contributions of your spokespeople all reflect on the professionalism of your campaign. Journalists do not tolerate sloppy press releases. They file them in the bin. MPs are inundated by letters from 'outraged' constituents. You might consider the latest actions of your local authority to be 'an abomination', but your MP is unlikely to be moved by unnecessarily intemperate language.

Getting your message into the local and national media is a crucial part of your communications strategy. As a group you should decide on one person to be the press officer. They will become a point of contact for the media and should be confident in talking to the press both on and off the record. Your press officer should be well-briefed, in other words, familiar with their campaign's key aims and objectives. They should be available to comment and conscious of journalists' deadlines. This section outlines the media opportunities available and the ways you can try to get your campaign covered.

Types of media

There is a wide range of media to approach these days. They are all competing to cover the same stories and potentially have lots of air time or pages to fill. Think about all the different types of media you want to reach – not just the national press; for example, consider:

- **Local daily and weekly newspapers:** they have high readerships and are influential. Do not overlook your locals. It is estimated that more than eight out of ten (83%) of all British adults read a local newspaper and over one-third (37%) of those do not read a national. Local newspapers are read by the local community and decision-makers alike. 'Councillors devour the local press. They read every word and quote it back,' says one campaigner. There is a range of ways to get into your local papers including letter writing, photo opportunities and selling in a news story or a feature.

- **Local radio stations:** there are over 300 local commercial radio stations alone reaching an estimated 27 million listeners, or 56% of all adults. They have a mix of news programmes, phone-ins, community news sections and discussion programmes. Doing your research and finding the right programmes for your campaign will impress journalists; all too often people call up with little more knowledge than the name of the radio station.

- **Television news:** the programmes that follow the national news throughout the day. There are big audiences, but few slots are available and your story will need a strong visual emphasis.

- **Internet:** if people want to find out what is happening on their doorstep then their first instinct is no longer to pick up a local newspaper or switch on a radio or a TV. They will be more likely to go online and 'Google' their chosen subject. Many of us get our news, pursue our interests and keep up with our enthusiasms online. We consider online campaigning separately in chapter 6.

Many websites, from BBC online to daily newspapers and local websites, urge readers to have their say. Being a part of these forums and discussions is a useful way to make your voice heard.

Also consider that many campaigns exist pretty much solely in cyberspace these days – see later in this chapter.

- **Specialist publications:** trade magazines might seem narrow in focus and have small circulations, but don't disregard them. They might be the only publications that will follow the details of your argument, plus they are more likely to be read by decision-makers.

The right story for the right media

Local media love local stories, especially those with a human interest angle. National media will not be interested in a local story (and local media might not be that interested in a national campaign). Do your research. Find out the name of the journalist before you ring in (what is it they write about, and why would your story be relevant?). Always consider the relevance of your story to the journalist you are contacting. If you get it right, you can make yourself a valuable resource to the journalist as they can come to depend on you as a reliable and efficient source of information. Get it wrong more than once and you could soon become a pain.

Send a press release well in advance if you want the media to attend an event, come to a demonstration, or cover your story. You also need to be aware of deadlines for weekly and daily publications and programmes and find out the best times to phone. Don't ring up on reporters' deadlines – it's too late and they will find it irritating (for dailies this is at the end of the day, about 5pm). For a weekly local paper, you need to contact the reporter at least three days before press day and on a national daily, one to two days before going to press. For broadcast media, one to ten days depending on whether it is a feature requiring some advanced planning (maximum notice is needed) or a short mention in the news section. An embargo on your press release can be useful if you want to tell the media about your event or news in advance, but don't want them to publish it before a certain date. To do this write, for example, 'Embargoed until

12 noon on 23 April 2008' at the very top of your press release.

What makes a good story

- **Be clear about what you want to communicate.** Distil your story into three key messages.

- **Keep it fresh.** First and foremost, journalists are interested in something new to write about. The story of your campaign must therefore develop. The incinerator being built at the end of the road is news only once. Then the story must progress. Are the public being consulted adequately? How will the proposals contribute to carbon emissions when national government is formulating its carbon reduction policy on the issue, etc?

- **Think of pictures.** Editors will want strong visual images and so always have photographs available if possible.

- **Find case studies.** Personal experiences work well. Have case studies lined up. Find people who are happy to talk about how your campaign concerns them and make sure they are readily available and primed on the key messages.

- **Consider other pages.** There are plenty of opportunities to get your story covered in the media, not just the news pages. Consider feature stories. They have longer lead-in times – three to six weeks for the nationals and locals. Also consider the letter pages and good photographs that tell a story in their own right (i.e. a photo with a caption).

- **Celebrity support.** Finding the right celebrity with a genuine interest and commitment to your cause can go a long way to securing media coverage. Research pays off. You will need to find a celebrity with a special interest in your campaign. Persuade them to sign up, give their time for interviews, take part in photo opportunities or attend events. You will need to be clear about what you want from them. In some cases they may ask for expenses to be covered and you need to consider the cost implications. Support from local DJs, local broadcasters, sports personalities or your local MP can add an extra dimension to your media story.

Case studies are one of the most important elements of an effective press campaign, and they are often overlooked. They illustrate your issue and are of great interest to the journalist who will always want the human interest angle. Ensure you have people who are prepared to talk to the media about their experiences and are prepared well in advance. Make sure that reporters are aware of the availability of case studies through a press release or follow-up call. If the journalist chooses to run your story it is likely that they will need to talk to people quickly – make sure your case studies are contactable (include mobile phone numbers) and are willing to be photographed. Present a journalist with a willing case study, a photo and a news hook and basically you are doing their job for them (and they like that). Celebrity support will always help (see case study below).

CELEBS: XTRAORDINARY PEOPLE

Xtraordinary People, a campaign set up in 2004 to raise awareness of the need for dyslexia training in schools, actively sought out celebrities to help raise the profile of the cause. 'Having names like Richard Branson and Jamie Oliver undoubtedly helps, but I started out with no leads and no contacts,' says founder Kate Griggs. 'So never let that put you off. Everybody knows somebody who knows somebody.'

Is it difficult persuading the great and the good to back your group? 'My experience is that most rich or well-known people really want to give something back – you just have to ask,' she replies. 'Some people blank you and don't respond, but if you get one out of a hundred then you have succeeded.'

How to draft a press release

Journalists are inundated with press releases by post, fax and email every day. You are competing with national organisations and government as well as the national news agendas. Your press release needs to stand out from the crowd, and be clear and concise.

Everything you want to say should be captured in the first paragraph. The five 'Ws' are:

What?

Where?

Who?

When?

Why?

Your press release must capture what is happening, where it is happening, who is involved, when it is happening and why it is happening (see press release skeleton below).

PRESS RELEASE SKELETON

This outline covers the shape of an effective press release.

- Date (embargo details)
- Contact details
- Headline
- Opening paragraph:
  - keep it short;
  - say what is happening, who it involves, where it is happening and when;
  - should summarise the event/story.
- Second paragraph should expand on the first
- Short paragraph to explain importance or significance of event
- Interesting quote from person of importance
- Notes to editors:
  - research/footnotes;
  - further background;

- campaign background information; and
- weblinks to relevant sites.

See Appendix 3 for example press releases from Which?. Note how it fits the skeleton above. It is structured like a news story – short, concise and clear in its message. It contains a short quote and is supported by factual information. The body of the release (containing the news) fits on the first page and the notes to editor is on the second.

Media briefings and Q&A sheets

Media briefings and Q&A sheets can be very similar but have very different uses. The media briefing sheet is extra information about your campaign that isn't contained in the press release. Although the release outlines all the key points, the briefing can give more information on the context of your campaign. It can offer more facts and figures plus anecdotes and personal testimonies that may further interest the journalist.

A Q&A sheet is an essential document for all your campaign spokespeople. It details all your key messages and gives possible answers to some of the more difficult questions that may arise. It ensures that all spokespeople are sticking to the same message and you all have the facts at your fingertips. It can be very useful for those who are less used to doing interviews or public speaking. It can also include suggested responses to more difficult questions relating to your campaign.

Pitching a story

Once you have drafted the press release you need to ensure it reaches the right people. Journalists are bombarded constantly by press releases and you are competing with others to get your story covered. Emailing your press release, faxing or putting it in the post is no guarantee that the journalist will even read it. Be a step ahead by knowing your chosen media, what they are interested in, what would be relevant to them and what you can add by talking to them directly. Again, be aware of the importance of deadlines and don't ring when a journalist is on a deadline.

> **TOP TIPS**
>
> - Find the right contact.
>
> - Know the lead times and deadlines.
>
> - Build a relationship with your local journalists.
>
> - Make sure you have all the information the journalist may need when you call, including contact details of your spokespeople and case studies.
>
> - If you don't have all the information the journalist needs, call back, but do it quickly.
>
> - Make a follow-up phone call to check that your press release has got to the journalist.

Preparing for interviews

The principles of being a good interviewee are the same across TV, radio and newspapers. Here is a checklist for making the most of your interview opportunities:

- **Prepare.** What are the three main points you want to make? Have some brief notes, but not reams of paper as you may confuse yourself and rustling paper does not sound good on radio. You won't be able to have notes for TV.

- **Research.** Find out if the interview is live or pre-recorded, what the first question will be so you can rehearse your answer (if possible), and if other people are taking part in the interview (are they local representatives that directly oppose your view and will you have an effective right of reply?).

- **Leave time.** Don't arrive in a rush and feeling flustered.

- **Dress appropriately.** Avoid 'noisy' jewellery (such as bangles on table tops) for radio or busy, patterned clothes for TV.

- **Turn off your mobile.** Nothing is more annoying and

embarrassing than an ill-timed phone call.

- **Pre-empt tricky questions.** The likelihood is they won't come up, as interviews on the whole are very short with only a few questions. You are not a politician being grilled by John Humphrys on the BBC Radio 4's *Today* programme.

Things go wrong. If you make a mistake, take a deep breath and start again.

Writing to the papers

Letter writing is often considered to be less effective than news coverage, but the letters page can be a useful way to highlight debate around your campaign.

Successful letter writing needs the following elements:

- **Keep it local.** If a campaign is doing well in a local paper, it is something decision-makers will take notice of.
- **Be brief.** Like all good publicity materials, keep it short and to the point.
- **Use own experience.** Personalise your letter with real-life experiences or anecdotes as well as the key messages of your campaign. Highlight how your MP has or has not helped you.
- **Keep it simple.** Don't assume your audience knows the issues.
- **Don't hector.** Make sure the tone is right; no-one wants to be harangued.
- **Address correctly.** Contact your local paper to find out the correct person to send the letter to and whether they prefer email, post or fax.

If you are fortunate enough to have celebrity support, draft a letter that your celebrity can put their name to and which can be sent to all the local media. A news story can be the opinion of a well-known and respected person on a particular issue; for example, an actor fighting planning permission in their local village.

CASE STUDY: CAMPAIGN TO PROTECT RURAL ENGLAND

'We are in more or less permanent campaigning mode. A crucial part of our campaign is informing people of what is proposed by translating jargon into simple messages and pushing them out to the public.' Kevin Fitzgerald of the Hertfordshire branch of CPRE (Campaign to Protect Rural England).

How do you plan a press strategy? 'It needs to meet three objectives – establish a group's identity and aims, build a reputation as a reliable source of news, and provide information and comment on the issue. The best method of achieving these is by press releases. Letters to the editor are useful but have less impact. A press release delivers the story to the reporter saving them time.

In deciding which papers or media to use, spread the net wide. The wider the support the better and in any case the issue may be of interest in other areas. Become familiar with the style and prepare press releases accordingly.

The body of a press release needs to be short and eye-catching. Longer explanations (e.g. the minutiae of government policy) go in "Notes" or the "Q&A" section at the end of the press release. It is important to be available to take press calls. It is sometimes also advisable to call the news desk to check that the press release has arrived. Taking time to explain the background to a campaign is much appreciated by hard-pressed journalists. Eventually, they will seek you out for comment.'

How do you sustain long-term media interest? 'Keeping the pot boiling over a long period is essential. Ideally, at the beginning of the campaign there should be a plan for the regular release of information. Where this is not possible, campaigners need to be constantly aware of publicity opportunities. These could be in another press article which has some bearing on the campaign, a speech by a politician, or another angle on the issue. At this stage letters to the editor are useful, as are "open" letters to, for example,

MPs. The emergence of climate change as an issue gave a new line for long-standing campaigns against airport expansions.

Finally, one should adopt a positive attitude to the media, regarding them as part of the team, with them helping the group and the group helping them to meet mutual objectives.'

Other campaigning techniques

Petitions

A petition is a clear and short campaign statement which is circulated online or on paper and signed by as many people as possible. One report shows that signing petitions is the most popular form of taking part in charity campaigns with almost two-thirds (61%) of people signing one in the previous year – this compares with smaller numbers of people writing to MPs (13%) or taking part in a demo (8%) (nfpSynergy's *Campaigning and the Public Report*, 2006). Petitions can be sent to decision-makers to show the level of support for your campaign. At a local government level, the petition is a tried and tested way of demonstrating public support to alert your councillor to what's going on and might even trigger a debate in the council chamber. If you get a significant number of names, it may be of sufficient interest to the press to become a story in its own right. You can set up a photo opportunity recording the presentation of the petition to the person or organisation you are petitioning. If you get permission from the people who sign your petition, you could send them more information or updates on your campaign.

How to draft a petition

You need a short and clear statement which should be easy for people to agree or disagree with quickly. If it is too long, people won't take the time to read it through and are therefore less likely to sign. Provide space for people to sign and add their name, address and email and a box to tick if they would like to receive more information about your campaign. Make lots of copies and divide them among your campaign supporters to distribute. Online petitions can also gain a lot of support. Email your supporters and ask them to sign up online to support your campaign.

An online petition called the People's Petition (see www.peoplespetition.org.uk), backed by groups defending animal testing, became a key part of the coalition's campaign when the then Prime Minister Tony Blair added his name. It was for the large part an anonymous petition set up by the Coalition for Medical Progress and attracted more than 20,000 signatures. 'That was certainly a big boost to the campaign,' says Tom Holder, of Pro-Test (see chapter 6).

When Tony Blair was Prime Minister, Downing Street launched its e-petitions site so that you can set up your own petition on its website saving you a visit to Number 10. It proved an instant hit for online activists and to the government's embarrassment, one of the first big shows of feeling was a petition opposing its 'pay-as-you-drive' scheme for motorists, which attracted 1.8 million signatures. That itself represented a massively successful campaign. The Conservatives even suggested a system where 'if enough people sign an online petition in favour of a particular motion, then a debate is held in Parliament, followed by a vote, so that the public know what their elected representatives actually think about the issues that matter to them'. However, it also sparked a debate as to the value of online activism. Sceptics would say that the readily available nature of the e-petition, as well as its ease of use, devalues its worth and represents a lazy form of campaigning.

To find out more visit http://petitions.pm.gov.uk/. For more information on petitioning your MP see fact sheet P7 on the Parliament website at www.parliament.uk.

Campaign materials

Think about the look of your campaign – posters, leaflets and postcards are a simple way to get your message out to a wider audience. Read Liberty's *Your Right to Peaceful Protest – A guide* at

Appendix 6 for further guidance on the formalities that you need to follow. They are useful calling cards which can be sent to people you are writing to, or handed out when signing a petition.

Keep any publications clear and concise. Stick to a few key messages; too much detail will put people off. Make the most of the design and print skills available to you from members of the campaign team.

The quality of any campaign materials will reflect the professionalism of your campaign. It is not expensive paper or pretty images but the actual content and layout. If your flyers look shoddy, then they will have a negative impact. Stick to plain English using concise and simple language and a few key messages, so the outsider knows exactly what your campaign is about, where they can find out more and who to contact for further information. Consider gimmicks such as Gordon Brown masks – they might be relatively expensive, but they can make a huge impact at a demo and garner much press coverage.

A campaign postcard or Christmas card is both an effective way of lobbying decision-makers to show strength of feeling and a way of actively involving your supporters. Postcards are most effective when handwritten, and a great way of using constituency links by encouraging your supporters to target their own MPs. Each card should have:

- a striking design;
- a campaign message on the back;
- the address of the person to receive the card;
- space for a campaigning message; and
- your logo.

How far does your money go?

Budget	£250	£500	£1,000
A4 leaflets – (s/s) – 130 gsm gloss	2,000	4,200	9,000
A5 promotional flyers – (d/s) – 170 gsm silk	625	1,475	3,500
A6 postcards – (d/s) – 350 gsm silk	1,000	2,600	5,750
A3 posters – (s/s) – 130 gsm gloss	325	800	2,000
A4 case study – (d/s) – 250 gsm silk	500	1,250	2,800
Gordon Brown masks*	333	666	1,333

s/s = single-sided
d/s = double-sided
From Everyday Print
*Priced separately, 4Print and Design, Brighton

Publicity stunts

These are one-off activities with the aim of attracting the media. They can take any form. Think creatively and, above all, visually.

CASE STUDY: SURFERS AGAINST SEWAGE

Surfers Against Sewage, the Marine Conservation Society and the British Naturist campaigners teamed up on Brighton beach to promote the 'No butts on the beach!' event, asking smokers to dispose of their cigarette ends responsibly and keep our beaches 'butt-free'. The prospect of campaigners appearing 'butt naked' with the slogan 'No butts on the beach' daubed across their naked bottoms got the press out.

Let the media know what you are planning in advance. If they don't turn up, it's always worth a chase-up call on the day, especially if you are causing quite a stir among passers-by. Remember they might be interested in the photos after the event.

Public meetings

There are three kinds of meeting your campaign may want to organise:

1. public meetings designed to deliver a message or to call for support;

2. general campaign meetings that you could make open to the public; and

3. internal, or private meetings held to discuss campaign policy and management affairs.

All meetings should follow the same basic structure and be organised in such a way as to ensure that the people attending clearly understand what the purpose of the meeting is. They should be provided with, preferably in advance, an agenda about key points of the meeting. Notes of the meeting should be taken and a report made to your management committee. Even the most informal, impromptu meetings should be recorded if they are to be approved and any action taken.

- **Advance warning.** You will need to get dates into people's diaries at the earliest opportunity. If you are meeting frequently, make it a regular date (e.g. the first Tuesday in every month) rather than agree a date which is convenient to all (which will inevitably lead to countless email exchanges).

   Let people know:

   - who is going to attend or who should attend the meeting;

   - what the purpose of the meeting is or why it is being held;

   - where the meeting will be held;

   - when the meeting will be held; and

   - how the meeting will proceed (e.g. Q&A session, presentations and then general discussion).

- **Agenda for the meeting.** You should always prepare an agenda. It enables the chair to follow an agreed structure and to ensure that everything that people were expecting to be covered is, in fact, covered. For a typical agenda, see over. Some of the items may appear rather formal, but each one has its use. It may seem odd for an informal group meeting around a coffee table to follow an agenda; it makes sense when you want to recall certain points discussed at that meeting at a later date.

IPSWICH LITTER CLEARANCE GROUP

Agenda

Meeting 7.30 pm, 2 December

at: Friends' Meeting House, Pembroke Road, Ipswich

1. Introductions
2. Apologies
3. Chair's report
4. Approval of minutes arising on meeting of 2 October
5. Matters arising from the minutes of 2 October
6. Items for current meeting (Chair's report)

    Campaign

    Council

    Next steps
7. Membership update (Secretary's report)
8. Financial report (Treasurer's report)
9. Any other business
10. Next meeting details: 7.30 pm on 2 February at Friends' Meeting House

---

You should circulate the agenda for your forthcoming meeting at least two weeks in advance, together with the minutes of the previous meeting.

For more formal meetings, such as the group's AGM, it may be necessary to comply with a formal notice period. This will almost certainly be the case for a limited company (see chapter 1).

- **Attendance register.** It is important to have a record of everyone attending. Ensure that whoever attends signs an attendance sheet so that you know who has come along (adapt the sample contact sheet provided in chapter 1 as appropriate). Take names and other details on the door as people arrive, or circulate an attendance sheet during the meeting. If someone takes the trouble to attend your public meeting, they are showing a high level of motivation and could become an invaluable supporter. Don't let this opportunity slip through your fingers; ask them to say why they are there, ask if they want to be involved and how best to contact them (email addresses, mobile numbers and landlines). Your chair can remind people to complete the sheet during the meeting. Knowing who and how many people attended your meeting will help you gauge the level of local concern. A record of the numbers might also generate a news story in itself. Your press release could start, 'Last night over 80 people attended a public meeting at the village hall, expressing their concerns about ...'

- **Running the meeting.** Your chair must ensure that the meeting:

  - runs according to the agenda and covers all the items listed on it;

  - keeps to time; and

  - provides an opportunity for people to speak (as appropriate).

  There is a fine balance between allowing people the opportunity to have their say and losing control of a meeting. An experienced chair will keep a firm hand on the tiller. Ultimately, it's your meeting and you need to ensure that it fulfils its purpose, for example, to take a key decision on a campaign issue, to listen to concerns, etc. It is the chair's job to keep the meeting focused and keep to the agenda.

  If materials or published reports are being discussed at the meeting, then ensure that there are spare copies or summary reports made available for attendees to read and consider at the meeting.

- **Taking minutes.** It is essential that someone, normally the group's secretary, is responsible for taking minutes of the meeting. This job is to take contemporaneous meeting notes, and ensure minutes are typed up and completed in order to be approved and signed off. The model constitution (see Appendix 2) provides that it is a task for the group's secretary to take and keep minutes of all meetings. Remember that for public meetings any minutes should be made available for public disclosure at a later date.

Ensure that any steps agreed to be carried out at the meeting are put in place sooner rather than later. It is easier to continue the momentum for any particular action agreed at the meeting and to recall any points made at a meeting while it is fresh in everyone's mind.

Ensure that any record or minutes of the meeting are drafted, approved and then circulated to the attendees or publicised (if appropriate) as agreed. If your campaign has a website, it may be that you can agree to publish minutes of any public meeting on your site. However, you should remember to tell attendees of the meeting that minutes or a note of the meeting will be published there.

Holding a public meeting

There are various types of meeting:

- a speaker meeting, where representatives of different interest groups come to discuss the issue;
- a hustings or Question Time-style meeting where local politicians or decision-makers are invited to answer questions from the floor on a particular issue;
- a campaign meeting, where the public are invited to come and hear about a particular issue and your group's concerns.

Decide on your speakers. Prepare a brief on what is expected, how much of their time is required, and what you would like them to focus their presentation on. Consider your agenda, allowing for people arriving late. Ask your main speakers to speak for a short slot (say, ten minutes only) and make sure they stick to it and allow lots of time for questions.

Draft a flyer or poster. Put it up where your target audience is likely to go (e.g. hospital, playground, local notice boards, etc).

Prepare for unforeseen circumstances. There are lots of things that can go wrong at public meetings. Speakers may pull out or too few people may turn up. Others may also turn up who disagree with your campaign and may be hostile to you and your speakers. If you have a contingency plan (including alternative speakers) covering what to do in these circumstances, you will be able to manage potential difficulties more easily.

Always write and thank speakers afterwards.

If the meeting is a management committee meeting, then, unless your constitution provides otherwise, the minutes should be circulated to the group's committee officers and all of its members.

Protests, demos and marches

The point of a demonstration is to raise awareness of the campaign and give your supporters a voice. Nothing illustrates the strength of feeling better than a large number of supporters with placards and banners on the street. But be mindful of the amount of disruption that a demonstration can cause. An ill-tempered meeting outside your town hall could cause your group more harm than good. The events should be well-publicised in advance. The event could comprise:

* a short march;
* speeches;
* distribution of leaflets;
* press coverage; and/or
* handing in a petition.

If you are planning a demo:

- ensure you have enough supporters;
- consider what permission you might need;
- arrange for leaflets and placards;
- alert the press; and
- arrange speakers.

If you are organising a public meeting in the local pub, or a march down the high street on a busy Saturday afternoon, or a demo outside the town hall, you need to be aware of what you legally can and can't do. Peaceful protest might be a cherished part of our democratic society, but the legal right to protest was only introduced by the Human Rights Act 1998. As the civil rights group Liberty points out, that right is not absolute and there are a number of laws that can effectively curtail your rights. The recent concern of politicians about anti-social behaviour, as well as the threat of terrorism, means the right to protest has been weakened, whilst at the same time the police have been given greater powers to restrict the actions of demonstrators.

See Appendix 6 for *Your Right to Peaceful Protest – A guide* by Liberty (which includes guidance on leafleting, petitions and putting up posters). See also chapter 8 for an outline of the law on requests for advance notice to the police and in some cases approval for certain demonstrations and public assemblies.

CHAPTER 5

Dealing with decision-makers

'It's a matter of trying to make sure what you do causes the cost of complying with your demands to be less than the cost of ignoring you.'

Owen Espley, Friends of the Earth

The effective campaigner needs to know their way around local and national government. It might be that the very substance of your campaign is the withdrawal of a much-loved service by your local authority (e.g. a care home for the elderly) or, alternatively, it could be the introduction of a fiercely opposed one (e.g. a new smoke-belching incinerator on your doorstep). Local campaigns are local politics.

If the target of your campaign is a company (or perhaps you are objecting to the proposals of both your council and a developer), you will also need to understand what makes the business tick. Unreasonable opposition to corporate aspirations is unlikely to get you any further than antagonising your target. You will need to understand the competing internal and external forces on a business. You could appeal to its better nature. For a business, appearing to work with your demands could be an effective way of demonstrating its commitment to corporate responsibility within the community. A company can be very sensitive to any issues that adversely affect its reputation. In these days of 'corporate social responsibility', big business doesn't like to be seen to be riding roughshod over the feelings of the communities in which it is based. For the effective campaign, the message is that a policy of intelligent engagement with business is a best first step rather than all-out war.

Similarly, we live in a democratic society and the starting point has to be that your council or government is working on your behalf. Your first assumption should be that government (local or national) is not working to further its own ends or ambitions – although it may seem like this at times. It is important to bear this basic principle in mind when dealing with your council, MP or MEP, and, for example, if you and other residents are suffering a local noise nuisance, it is the responsibility of the council's environmental health department to resolve the matter. You, as residents, should not have to be left trying to sort the problems out.

You need to identify the key decision-makers and the best route of communication in order to raise your concerns. You should always build constructive relationships, if you can, with community leaders, businesspeople and politicians in your area who can assist your cause. A sympathetic non-executive director, councillor, MP or MEP can open doors which might otherwise be closed to you and your supporters. Unsurprisingly, an antagonistic relationship can impede process.

We now live in a culture of 'open government' – at least, that's what our politicians would like us to believe. An unhealthy combination of political apathy on our part and the arcane structures of local politics mean that some democratic institutions seem closed off to many of us. However, lobbying our elected representatives, whether they are local councillors, MPs or MEPs, is a vital way of getting your campaign message across. This chapter covers how business engages with campaigns as well as explaining the key political institutions at a local, national and European level. It will also identify the key politicians and staff that you should contact as well as shine light on the political processes in which you need to be involved. Your group might want to appoint a government liaison officer or one person who will be point of contact for lobbying issues.

> **CHAPTER OVERVIEW:**
>
> - Identifying the decision-makers
> - Business
> - Local government
> - National government
> - The European Union

Identifying the decision-makers

There are four key questions that you can ask yourself to identify what the National Council for Voluntary Organisations (NCVO) calls the 'roots of influence':

1. Who's the campaign target?
2. How much influence do you and your allies have over the target?
3. What and who influences the campaign target?
4. What are the best ways for you to reach your target?

These questions involve a consideration of what makes an institutional target tick, be they political or corporate. The NCVO takes the view that all too often campaigners 'mistakenly assume that because they occupy the moral high-ground…change will inevitably occur'. It is not as simple as that.

A useful place to start here is to draw an 'influence map', which identifies all the players who might have a bearing on the policy processes that relate to a particular issue. Cast your net wide. MPs will be influenced by other MPs, constituents such as yourselves, and parliamentary groups, as well as the wider business community. If you draw on the resources of your wider support base at this point, the chances are that they might have access to people of influence within the chain.

The 'influence map' will help you prioritise those players that will have the greatest impact on your campaign. Some might seem beyond your reach. If you have previously not had any contact with a group, for example, the Confederation of British Industry, but they would have the greatest impact on your campaign, then you might need to go through a secondary route to reach your target, which could be, for example, a trade union. The example of an influence map below was prepared for the National Fire Sprinkler Campaign, which was calling for superstores to be obliged to fit sprinkler systems. The law has been changed to make sprinklers compulsory.

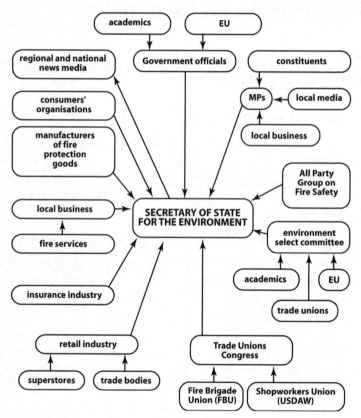

Source: NCVO

Business

There are two factors that will determine a business's willingness to take notice of your campaign. Firstly, the culture of that company and, critically, the extent to which it engages externally with the outside world. Secondly, its business and the extent to which your issues are central to the company's business. To help illustrate the point see the diagram below devised by Jayanti Durai, a specialist in corporate public relations.

ISSUE IS CORE TO BUSINESS

AIM: Position issue as a threat to future profits

TARGET: Company Board and investors

TACTICS: AGM demonstrations or questions by shareholders Questions/petitions to ethical funds (SR) to disinvest

AIM: Work with company to better manage issue

TARGET: Corporate responsibility team to raise internally with Corporate Affairs, Risk and Board

TACTICS: One-to-one meetings, town hall meetings

CLOSED TO EXTERNAL ENGAGEMENT ON THIS ISSUE

AIM: Create noise, build awareness, strengthen numbers of concerned people to force engagement

TARGET: Local MPs, prospective MPs, Councillors, NGOs

TACTICS: Petitions, one-to-one briefings, stalls at local fairs, posters

AIM: Improve company's understanding of impact on local community

TARGET: Community Officer HR or local MD

TACTICS: One-to-one meetings, town hall meetings

ISSUE IS NOT CORE TO BUSINESS

- Evaluate core business strategy in relation to your issue. Does your issue affect core strategy? What is the company trying to achieve? Check the company website and read the annual report.

- Evaluate nature of company engagement. Check to see what level of corporate social responsibility (CSR) there is and how the company engages with individuals and groups who have a direct interest in the issue. Check the company's CSR if it has one.

- Plot the company on the graph above to identify the first course of action, with the ultimate aim of engaging with the company to encourage action.

- By engaging with the company rather than confronting it, a longer-term understanding of community needs will be developed. This then helps future similar issues.

You may find that a direct approach might well bear fruit in the case of a company that isn't engaging with your campaign even though it is directly relevant to the business. This may be because investors see your campaign as a potential business risk, explains Jayanti Durai, who is also head of corporate responsibility at the London-based PR firm Munro & Forster. If your campaign falls into the category where the issues aren't central to the business, nor does the company play a part in the community, then you need to take the campaign to local councillors, MPs, MEPs and NGOs to force this up its agenda.

Do not assume that local business will be in opposition to your campaign (see below).

CASE STUDY: THE MODBURY TRADERS

In 2006 Rebecca Hosking, a wildlife camerawoman, was filming in the Pacific on a remote Hawaiian atoll for the BBC. It was not the paradise that she was expecting; instead, Hosking was shocked by the level of plastic bag pollution. 'It really affected me,' she later told the press. 'I have never cried behind a camera before. I'm not a blubby person. But it broke my heart to see animals entangled in plastic, albatrosses dying in plastic, dolphins trailing plastic and seals with their noses trapped in parcel tape roll. The sea is now like a trash can and the plastic is there forever.' In less than a month, Hosking persuaded all 43 shopkeepers in Modbury, a small West Country town, to replace the plastic bag with reusable cloth bags. It is the first plastic bag free town in the UK and has kick-started numerous other local campaigns.

Why was this issue so persuasive? 'Rebecca invited the 43 traders to come to the gallery to watch her film,' says Sue Sturton, who runs the Brownston art gallery. 'The film really brought home to me the damage that plastics do in the marine environment and how long they take to degrade even if they are biodegradable. Everything that we have created that is plastic is theoretically still around us. I was shocked. We were all won over by the fact that Modbury was a small town and this was something a small town could do. We really felt that we could make a difference.'

What was the cost to business? Sandra Everett, head of marketing at the Plymouth and South West Co-operative, reckons the cost of plastic bags was about £2,250 a year whereas the price of the new environmentally friendly corn starch bags were going to cost as much as £25,000 a year. 'We needed to bring in a charge to recoup some of the cost ourselves which would also lead the consumer to focus on whether they needed the bags,' she says. 'The whole idea is to reduce, reuse and recycle.' There had to be agreement on this among the traders. 'We couldn't have someone giving bags away and someone else charging 25p,' Everett adds. All 43 traders offer the biodegradable cornstarch alternatives at 5p a bag or encourage customers to bring their own.

Was there any resistance from the Plymouth and South West Co-operative to the campaign? 'No. We've been involved from the start. I think Rebecca thought because we're part of a bigger group that she would find more resistance from us; however, we are an independent society and I would like to think that we are forward-thinking and we are interested in how to protect the environment. The only resistance that we offered was to make sure that it was all done properly and that any bags that were going to be substituted were environmentally safe and also people safe,' says Everett.

What advice would the traders offer other would-be campaigners about getting business on their side? 'The worst thing you can do is tell people that they should do it,' says Sturton. 'Human nature tends to resist when we are told to do something.' Since the success of the Modbury campaign the Plymouth and South West Co-operative has been approached by other towns. Sandra Everett says that they are constantly being asked by other local groups to provide free bags which she argues is unrealistic (it could cost £25,000 per store every year and the chain has 4,600 stores).

Who to contact

There are numerous points of first contact for campaigners to target, principally the:

- chief executive;
- chair;
- board of directors;
- press officers;
- employees (including representative groups, such as trade unions); and
- shareholders.

If you are concerned about a company's behaviour, then the first point of contact should be that company itself. You can write directly to the chief executive and the directors. If you're not sure who the directors are, contact the company directly or request the information from Companies House. It is a good idea to send your letter by special delivery to ensure that you have proof that the letter has been received.

It is well worth researching the background of the chief executive and the board of directors, in particular non-executive directors, for example, through online newspaper archives. A non-executive director is a company director who attends board meetings, gives advice to the company and carries all the potential liabilities of other directors, but doesn't work full-time. They can act as the conscience of a business organisation, providing checks and balances on the executive directors. The idea is that they should be seen to be independent from the company and capable of exercising objective and independent judgment.

It is also worth checking out a company's CSR policy, which could be available online, in its annual report or by request. Many commentators dismiss such policies as PR spin, but nonetheless 'CSR' is now a multi-billion-pound industry and it isn't easy these days to find a major company whose annual report doesn't extol its credentials. 'Go through the policy, check out the website and try to relate statements made in the press to their actions so you can hold them to account,' comments Owen Espley, corporate power campaigner at Friends of the Earth. If the evidence of your campaign demonstrates that a company is doing exactly what it is holding itself out not to be doing in its CSR report or press interviews with its chief officers, then that gives you powerful leverage. Certainly, if you can divert the energies of the chief executive away from running the business to deal with your issues then that the company is forced to take you seriously.

'Do not oppose for the sake of opposing it,' advises Sue Stapely, who specialises in advising businesses and organisations on reputational issues. 'Instead of just saying, "we want our village green to remain a greenfield site and we don't want a supermarket" you need to structure a range of arguments as to why it would be reputationally damaging not to act, why it would be to the benefit of the community to comply with your aims, and then maybe cite a compromise with which the community and the activists could live and which would give some kind of elegant solution to the commercial entity as well. It's always a preferred lobbying tactic to come up with some kind of compromise solution which gives them a bit of leeway and looks as though you both have shifted your ground a bit.'

Often campaigners are told to speak to the press office. As Espley says, their job can be to 'manage activism'. That's not what you want. Appealing directly to the employees (possibly with the support of a trade union) can have a strong impact. It's not easy for a business to live with an unhappy workforce.

Shareholder activism

'In the last 20 years there has been increasing emphasis placed on the value of non-tangible assets and the brand has become increasingly important,' says Owen Espley, corporate power campaigner at Friends of the Earth. 'By trying to piggyback on the brand and making the brand synonymous with dirty behaviour the campaigner gets real leverage and that affects the value of the company with shareholders.' If you own shares in a company, that can provide a direct route to furthering the aims of your campaign. Such shareholder activism has been bolstered through the Companies Act 2006 which means that the primary responsibility of the company is to its shareholders. The following has been adapted from the Corporate Responsibility (CORE) Coalition and The Trade Justice Movement's *Act Now! A campaigner's guide to the Companies Act.*

- **How are companies accountable?** Companies are required by law to be accountable to their shareholders. Shareholders also have certain powers; for example, they can:
  - get more detailed information about what the companies are up to;
  - vote at the AGM over crucial issues (such as hiring and firing the directors);
  - join with other shareholders to bring a resolution at an

AGM in relation to the company's activities;

- in certain cases, bring a legal challenge for breach of duty if the directors have failed to take into account those activities.

- **How do you become a shareholder?** It is not expensive. You can buy as little as one share in a company and this can be done through brokers at most high street banks in the bigger branches, or over the telephone or online. Choose your broker with care as the commission that banks charge does vary significantly. To buy shares online or over the phone you will need to open a special account for your shares only. Alternatively, if you know a shareholder the simplest way is to get someone to transfer one of their shares to you. Ask them to transfer the share as a gift and then you will not pay any brokers' fees. All you need is a stock transfer form, which you can ask the company to provide or simply download it from the Internet. Another option is to go to the AGM of the company and vote by asking a like-minded shareholder to sign a proxy form, which is sent out to shareholders ahead of the AGM, which enables you to vote.

- **What can shareholders do?** Shareholder resolutions are a powerful way of sending a message to company directors. These resolutions are actually proposals submitted by shareholders which are then put to a vote at the company's AGM. Resolutions often deal with environmental and social issues related to a company's behaviour and although they are normally defeated (by not getting enough votes) they have been influential in raising public awareness and changing corporate behaviour.

As to how to table a resolution – that can vary. You will possibly need the support of some major individual shareholders securing at least 5% of total voting rights, or 100 members each with a minimum £100 worth of shares. Ideally, the resolution should challenge the company's poor risk management or the absence of relevant policy, as large investors are more interested in how the company is managed rather than individual projects.

Institutional shareholders are typically pension firms or banks investing on behalf of a large number of smaller shareholders. They regularly meet with the company's office holders and can ask senior management about its activities.

It is likely that members of your campaign group belong to pension funds with shares in major companies listed on the stock exchange. Members can write to their fund trustees and ask what companies they invest in. According to EIRIS (the Ethical Investment Research Services) there are also about 90 'ethical' retail funds which have screening policies to rule out the likes of arms manufacturers and tobacco companies which also make assessments of environmental impact.

CASE STUDY: WAR ON WANT

Tesco came under considerable pressure in June 2007 to improve the plight of workers in Bangladesh who were paid 5p an hour to produce clothes for its British stores, as a result of a campaign by the anti-poverty group War on Want.

A resolution was proposed by Ben Birnberg, company secretary of the group, and this won support from more than 100 shareholders, including the Joseph Rowntree charitable trust, which holds close to a million shares. The resolution was supported by a Bangladeshi researcher, who interviewed workers who made Tesco clothes in the country's capital, Dhaka, for a War on Want report which showed employees were working 80 hours a week for just 5p an hour. 'Tesco prides itself on promoting core values and seeking to uphold labour standards in the supply chain,' Birnberg told the press. 'Yet our evidence shows Tesco keeps its prices low by exploiting workers in developing countries like Bangladesh. If Tesco is genuine about its ethical pretensions, why are its directors advising shareholders to vote down my resolution?'

The move generated national press coverage and dramatically raised the profile of the conditions of Bangladeshi workers.

Companies Act 2006

This legislation has been the result of years of campaigning from the likes of the Corporate Responsibility (CORE) Coalition and the Trade Justice Movement. Unlike previous company law, the Act means that a company must now consider the impact of its business on the community, employees and the environment.

Two key sections of the legislation highlight links between a company's financial performance and its social and environmental performance. These sections are:

- **Directors' duties** (Section 172). Company directors have a responsibility to consider the impact of their company on a range of social and environmental matters. Directors must consider issues relating to employees, suppliers, customers, the community and the environment.

- **Transparency** (Section 417). Publicly listed UK companies have a responsibility to report openly on their social and environmental risks and opportunities to their shareholders. Quoted companies will be required to produce an annual report called a 'business review' that includes information on their track record on, for example, the environment.

According to CORE and the Trade Justice Movement, these parts of the new Act provide 'a tool to help defend the rights of people and protect the environment against irresponsible corporate behaviour'. They argue that the legislation can also be used as an 'educational tool' to remind directors of their legal responsibilities; as a tool 'to strengthen the right of shareholders to demand ethical performance'; and as a 'legal tool' available to shareholders to bring companies to account through the courts. There is an example letter on the following page illustrating the use of the Companies Act to question corporate behaviour.

CORE and the Trade Justice Movement believe that a company should include in its business review the following types of information:

- For a mining company, details of a project in an area where the local indigenous community is seriously opposed (including the human rights implications of using private security forces).

- For a supermarket that has signed up to an ethical labour code, measures taken to ensure that the policies it has in place are actually being enforced.

- For a food manufacturing company, actions they are taking to ensure that ingredients such as palm oil are produced ethically and sustainably.

Model letter to the board of directors and/or chief executive:

Dear [name of directors/chief executive],

I am concerned that your company is [e.g. sourcing its goods from X]. As you may or may not be aware, some of the activities [e.g. of your suppliers] have been causing [e.g. environmental harm to the X community] through [describe the problem and refer to supporting evidence].

The Companies Act 2006 stipulates in Sections 172 and 417 respectively that you have a duty to take such issues into consideration and report on them [only include Section 417 reporting reference if the company is quoted on the stock exchange].

I do not believe that the above issues are currently being appropriately considered by your company and I am concerned about whether this may consequently be a breach of the Companies Act. This letter has been copied to the Secretary of State for Business, Enterprise and Regulatory Reform, who has responsibility to enforce the Act.

I look forward to hearing from you as soon as possible as to how you plan to manage the significant issues and ensure that your shareholders are made aware of them.

Yours faithfully,

For more information (including a copy of *Act Now! A campaigner's guide to the Companies Act*), see www.corporate-responsibility.org.

Local government

'I didn't have any experience of lobbying and I think that helped. My view was, "let's just go for it". MPs are a fantastic place to start because of all the things that they can do on your behalf if they really believe in what you're saying. My advice when it comes to dealing with MPs and ministers – keep bombarding them.'

Kate Griggs, Xtraordinary People

Structure

Local government in the UK is structured in the following ways.

Single-tier 'all-purpose' councils in Scotland, Wales and parts of England which are responsible for all local authority functions. In England these are the 36 metropolitan authorities, 33 London boroughs and 47 English shire unitary authorities. In Wales there are 22 unitary authorities and in Scotland 32.

Two-tier authorities. The remainder of England has a two-tier system in which two separate councils divide responsibilities between district and county council level. There are 34 county councils and 238 district councils in England. The former provides some services such as education, social services and trading standards, and the district councils carry out other services such as housing, environmental health, etc. County councils provide around 80% of the services in these areas.

There are also around 10,000 parish/town councils in England (they are called community councils in Wales). They are the first tier of local government and have some powers, such as maintaining bus stops and being consulted on planning applications as well as other activities for the benefit of the community.

Office holders

- **Mayors and chairs.** All local authorities have either a chair or a mayor as leader; in some cities they will be called Lord Mayors. Where an authority is a district council it will have a chair and where the authority is a borough or city council it will have a mayor or Lord Mayor as leader. Authorities can now opt for a directly elected mayor (under the Local Government Act 2000) after a referendum.

- **Councillors.** There are some 20,000 elected councillors representing local communities. The primary role of the councillor is to represent their local authority area; in other words, just like your MP they are there to represent you. They have a responsibility to communicate council policy and decisions to you, the people.

  The main duty of a councillor is to work on behalf of the community. Their workload involves:

  - council meetings;
  - committee meetings;
  - responding to letters and emails from local residents;
  - holding surgeries; and
  - meeting representatives from pressure groups and organisations.

  Except for members of the council's executive, most councillors are unpaid (although they do receive an annual allowance and expenses). Most councillors are members of political parties and stand for election as party candidates. These parties form voting groups in the council, with members of one party expected to vote the same way on each issue. In some councils, one party has a clear majority. In others, no party has overall control.

  Councillors are elected for a four-year term unless they are elected at a by-election, in which case they must stand again at the next election. They take part in making decisions that impact on their ward and throughout the council area; for example, they sit on council committees such as planning control, licensing, local voluntary organisation management, sitting on boards and as school governors.

Councillors also influence and review the council's policy and strategy. They can do this through their involvement in advisory groups and partnerships, interaction with executive members and as representatives on local community groups.

Councillors have always been required to examine the actions of the council, providing a check on the activities of the executive through what are known as 'call-in powers', monitoring and reviewing policy and scrutinising external bodies and agencies.

Local authorities are not just service providers, they act as regulators. When considering issues such as planning and licensing applications they are required to act independently. They are not subject to the party group whip and don't have to stick to the party line.

- **Officers.** Officers are the employees of the council who put policy into effect and organise the provision of services. Officers may also be delegated by councillors to make policy decisions. They are the local government equivalent of civil servants. They are led by a chief executive and senior managers who have been appointed directly by councillors.

CASE STUDY: MERTON PARENTS

'We wrote to every single councillor and put their contact details on our website with the aim of generating loads of emails for them. It is something you need to do. Most people are utterly clueless as to how local government works,' says Jackie Schneider, of the school dinners campaign Merton Parents for Better Food. 'Because we were causing such a stir, we had a lot of councillor interest and often they were school governors as well. They were quickly embarrassed and you could see they were agonising as to which way to jump – to defend school dinners or come over to us. Councillors, and governors, do a lot of boring stuff. I was surprised by how lacking in passion

> they were. Because our campaign was so passionate a lot of them were quite invigorated by it.'

How councils work

A council has a constitution which sets out the framework within which it conducts its business and makes decisions. It is not necessarily an easy read but will give an overview of:

- decision-making;
- council structures;
- procedural matters;
- roles of officers; and
- standards and ethical governance.

The full council meeting is known as 'the sovereign body of the council'. Full council is where all councillors meet to debate and take decisions and historically it received recommendations from various committees. The Local Government Act 2000 changed this and introduced a system that separated the decision-making executive from the monitoring and representative part of the council. The legislation was introduced to increase democratic accountability by establishing an identifiable executive. The three main structures available to councils now are:

1. an elected mayor with executive powers;
2. a leader and cabinet with executive powers selected from and by the council; or
3. an elected mayor with an appointed council manager.

This legislation means that the council's executive decision-making arrangements can come under one single political party. The executive mayor or cabinet is responsible for:

- agreeing new policy and the budget;
- conducting strategic service reviews; and
- implementing decisions of the full council.

Councils must allow for a system of checks and balances whereby non-executive councillors hold to account the performance of the executive. They are supposed to do this in a way which engages public debate. Overview and scrutiny arrangements have to reflect the political balance of the council and so committees should include members from all parties. The government has also proposed that each council should have a standards committee to make sure councillors stay on the straight and narrow.

Any decision or action taken by the council (whether taken by officers, committees or subcommittees) is taken by the council as a whole. If a decision is taken by an officer or a subcommittee, they must have delegated authority to take that decision. If not, the decision is unlawful. As the majority of council decisions are taken by delegated officers of committees it is always worth checking to see that it was done properly. Every council should publish its scheme of delegation.

Making contact

You have a number of options. There is no one way to raise a particular concern. The key is to find a sympathetic ear. Your options include:

- **Your electoral ward councillor.** The councillor in your local area might be your first port of call – and the most obvious. They are elected to represent your concerns and you have a right to tell them your opinions.

- **Other councillors.** Of course, you may contact any councillor, but there might be a councillor with a particular sympathy for your campaign.

- **Council officers.** Many administrative actions and decisions are taken by officers and so if you don't have a sympathetic councillor, or you think your issue can be better dealt with by another office holder, then contact them direct.

- **Committee chairs.** Find out if there is a committee on the particular issue you are concerned about and contact the person who chairs it.

Consider the timing. You need to check whether the council is likely to be having a meeting to discuss the issue. You need to be aware of what stage of the decision-making process the council has reached.

Contact your council or check out its website. Councils are legally obliged to provide a public register of the names and addresses of councillors, plus details of the committees they sit on. The website www.writetothem.com will identify your local councillors, your MP and your MEPs. All you have to do to access this information is enter your postcode.

You can write to your councillor, or attend a 'surgery', as councillors hold surgeries where they meet face-to-face with constituents in the same way as MPs do. You can attend council meetings which are generally open to the public unless they are classed as 'exceptional'. There might be an opportunity to speak at these meetings. Members of the public have no automatic speaking rights at council meetings. You will need to check out local arrangements.

You need to demonstrate that your concerns are reflected widely within the community in order to have the greatest impact with your councillor. Raising a petition is a traditional method of demonstrating a show of public support – see chapter 4.

Can I attend council meetings? Generally, yes. As mentioned above, almost all council meetings are open to the public unless there are reasons to exclude you. Usually this is when something commercially confidential is being discussed, or if matters that are legally sensitive are being considered. For example, the committee members could be using the council meeting to discuss with the council's lawyers whether or not they should take enforcement proceedings for unlawful development. In this case you would not be able to attend. However, the assumption should be that a meeting will be open to the public.

Notice of public meetings is required by law with the date, time, venue and agenda to be posted publicly five working days before the meeting takes place. A councillor may speak on your behalf, but they cannot vote unless they are a member of the committee concerned. Members of the public have no automatic speaking rights at council meetings. However, the majority of councils will allow you to speak. You should check with your council a few days before the committee meeting and ask for permission at that time. If you are given the opportunity to speak, it is likely to be limited to around three minutes. So be prepared to be direct and concise. Also, it is quite likely that the committee will only allow one speaker from any one group. If you are acting for a number of residents, or there are a number of groups with similar concerns, it will be worth arguing why each has justification for making separate representations to the committee and also discuss who will say what during their allotted time.

At a formal meeting, a record is made by council officers of the decisions taken, the background papers received and the reasons for a decision. These meeting minutes are available to members of the public.

- **Standing for election.** In England and Wales more than 21,000 people serve as councillors on local authorities. To stand as a councillor you must be 18 years of age or over and on the electoral register of the authority for which you wish to stand, or alternatively you must have worked in the local area for the last 12 months. Certain people are barred from standing for election and these include undischarged bankrupts, people convicted of corrupt or illegal electoral practices and people who within the last five years have been sentenced to more than three months' imprisonment.

  Single issue electoral candidates (as opposed to those representing a political party) have been an increasing feature on both the local and the national political stage. It was the anti-sleaze campaigner and former BBC war correspondent Martin Bell who inspired many other campaigners to have a go, standing against the Tory MP Neil Hamilton in 1997. Independent candidates have since been elected as mayors of Hartlepool and Middlesbrough. Dr Richard Taylor, a former hospital consultant, won the safe Labour seat of Wyre Forest with a majority of 17,000 in 2001. His victory led to a government moratorium on hospital closures and the introduction of new consultation procedures. He went on to become a member of the Parliamentary Health Select Committee.

For a particular example of a campaign engaging with local government, see Appendix 4 for Gay Brown's guide to the planning system. A local resident in Yiewsley, West London she was involved in a campaign against an application by Tesco. 'Being suddenly faced with the prospect of a supermarket can seem daunting,' she says. 'However, if you take it step-by-step you can get there. It isn't rocket science.'

CASE STUDY: DUMP THE DUMP

Dump the Dump is a Brighton-based campaign group fighting against proposals for a waste transfer station. 'We stood as independent candidates in the three wards surrounding the proposed site, one person in each ward,' says campaigner Jo Offer.

How? 'We paid our deposit, got ten nominees to vouch for each one of us and set about writing a manifesto a month before the election. We met nearly every evening for the first week and eventually distilled what is a huge, complex and often depressing subject into an easily digestible piece of literature. Then we got about 10,000 manifestos printed up with a few hundred posters.'

Why? 'Our aim was to show that the council and opposition councillors failed to help develop a method for handling waste. We all make rubbish, we all need to take responsibility for what we throw away and we should all be part of the solution. However, consultation on this was meaningless and 4,000 letters of objection meant nothing.'

Why stand for election? 'It was an opportunity to let people know that our campaign was still going strong, still enjoying local support and that the issue of how we dispose of our waste was one that the whole city needed to face. Our aim was for all political parties to keep the issue of waste on their campaign materials and we asked everyone, even those outside our three electoral wards, to question their local councillors on the local waste plan and its implications for the city over the next 25 years. It was a chance for us to explain that our campaign was not a NIMBY issue – no-one should have to live, work or go to school next to a dump. It will be a huge development in the middle of a densely residential area. One 44-ton lorry is expected every seven minutes of every day.'

How did your campaign go down? 'People responded with a mixture of incredulity ("Why would anyone want to be a councillor?"), support and relief that they had someone to vote for. We put tables in the street and leafleted our three wards twice but didn't canvass door-to-door. We made sure people knew they had a total of three votes and we explained that, if elected, we would approach decisions from a community perspective – something that was sorely lacking.'

What happened? 'We didn't get elected, but between us we had a respectable count (1,338 votes in total) and felt it was all worth it. Those of us who felt unheard got to have our say.'

For more information on local government, visit www.lga.gov.uk and to find out more about becoming a councillor, visit www.idea.gov.uk.

National government

Structure

The workings of Westminster are generally better understood than local government. Parliament is where all our laws are made and changed and it provides checks and balances on government. The business of Parliament takes place in the House of Commons and the House of Lords. Their work is mainly making laws, scrutinising the work of the government and debating issues. Generally, the decisions made in one House have to be approved by the other. In this way the two-chamber system acts as a check and balance.

- **House of Commons.** At the time of going to press, it is made up of 646 Members of Parliament (MPs). The party with the largest number of members in the Commons forms the government. MPs debate the political issues of the day and proposals for new laws. It is one of the key places where government ministers, such as the Prime Minister and the Chancellor, and the principal figures of the main political parties, work.

- **House of Lords.** It is the second chamber and plays an important part in revising legislation and keeping a check on government. It complements the House of Commons. Life peers currently make up the majority of total membership – at the end of 2007, about 646 out of 730. The power to appoint them belongs to the Crown, but in reality members are created on the advice of the Prime Minister. The titles of life peers end on death. There are only a small number of hereditary lords left (92); they are being phased out. In addition, a limited number of Church of England archbishops and bishops sit in the House. The House of Lords is also the Supreme Court of Appeal (see chapter 8) and the law lords (full-time professional judges) sit in the chamber.

Devolution

The UK Parliament at Westminster has devolved different powers to the Scottish Parliament, the National Assembly for Wales, and the Northern Ireland Assembly – in other words, decisions that Parliament used to control are now taken by these separate bodies. This could include matters to do with planning, the environment, local government, education, health and the law. Reserved powers are those decisions that remain with Parliament in Westminster. In each case, the legislation establishing the separate bodies determined which powers were devolved and which were reserved. For more information, see www.scotland.gov.uk, www.wales.gov.uk and www.niassembly.gov.uk.

How Parliament works

It has two main functions:

- **Debate.** Both Houses hold debates in which government policy, new laws and current issues are discussed. Debates are designed to assist MPs and Lords to reach an informed decision on a subject. Votes are often held to conclude a debate, which may involve passing or rejecting a proposed new law or simply registering opinion on a subject. All debates are recorded in Hansard, which is available online (or in print); see www.publications.parliament.uk/pa/pahansard.htm. It is searchable and can be a useful resource tool to find out what MPs and ministers have to say on any issue (although the www.theyworkforyou.com site is also useful as it is designed for, in its words, 'keeping tabs on your elected and non-elected representatives').

- **Legislation.** It is the government that introduces most proposals for new laws, or changes to existing laws, but not exclusively. They can come from an MP, Lord or even a member of the public. Before they can become law, both the House of Commons and House of Lords must debate and vote on the proposals. 'Bills' normally introduce new laws. To become law, a bill must be agreed by both Houses of Parliament. Either House can vote it down, in which case it will normally not become law – but there are exceptions. The Commons can pass the same bill in two successive years, in which case it can become law without the agreement of the Lords. The Queen has to approve all new laws (in other words, give 'Royal Assent') but it has not been withheld since 1708.

  There are different types of bill. Public bills relate to the law as it applies to the general population and are the most common type. Ministers propose the majority of public bills. Private Members' bills are a type of public bill introduced by MPs and

Lords who aren't government ministers. A minority of these bills become law, but even so they can work to increase the profile of an issue and can affect legislation indirectly. For more information, see fact sheet L2 on the Parliament website at www.parliament.uk/documents/upload/l02.pdf. Private bills are usually promoted by organisations, such as local authorities or private companies, to give themselves powers beyond, or in conflict with, the general law. Private bills only change the law as it applies to specific individuals or organisations, rather than the general public.

At each stage of a bill there will be opportunities to lobby your MP. It might be that because of their implication for you and your fellow campaigners as constituents you call upon MPs to try to change the substance of the proposed legislation (by putting down amendments). It is often possible to work with local charities or non-governmental organisations and make use of their greater campaigning resources. A postcard or letter-writing campaign can be an effective way of making your feelings understood (see chapter 4). You can allow for the letters/postcards to be customised and sent on to your own MP and other sympathetic MPs. This begins to create waves as MPs and their researchers are inundated with postcards prompting them to start looking into an issue.

For more information about how Parliament works, see www.parliament.uk.

What MPs can do for you

The public elects MPs to represent their interests in the House of Commons each representing a single constituency. They are there to represent you, whether you voted for them or not. MPs are involved in considering and proposing new laws, and can use their position to ask ministers questions about current issues. MPs split their time between working in Parliament, their constituencies, and with their political party. Some MPs from the ruling party become government ministers with specific responsibilities in certain areas, such as health or defence.

At Parliament MPs generally spend their time working in the Commons. This can include raising awareness of issues affecting their constituents, attending debates and voting on new laws. Most MPs are also members of committees, which look at issues in detail, from government policy and new laws, to wider topics such as human rights.

You can write to your MP via the House of Commons. All MPs have a Westminster office and if they are out of London their mail will be redirected to their constituencies. You can also email them – see the constituency locater service for their email addresses at www.parliament.uk/directories/hciolists/alms.cfm. The website www.writetothem.com has details for MPs, MSPs, Northern Ireland and Welsh Assembly members.

You can meet your MP at one of their regular surgeries. Details are usually advertised in the local press and posted in public libraries. The MP's secretary or local office will also be able to tell you when your MP will next be holding a surgery. If the House of Commons is sitting, you are allowed to go to the central lobby to see your MP, although it is best to make an appointment as they might be meeting other people.

To ensure that you make your point most effectively, contact your MP direct. They should be happy to meet you. Remember it isn't a question of their doing you a favour. MPs need to be seen to be at work in their own constituency, and local community groups like yours provide a big opportunity for them.

When discussing matters with your MP, stick to specific queries about your campaign and ask for realistic input from the MP. If it is a council matter they will probably know the councillors and will be able to talk to them about the issues. MPs will generally be more than happy to raise an issue with a government minister, put down parliamentary questions and possibly an Early Day Motion (see later). If you are organising a public event and your MP is supportive, then invite them.

MPs will generally be busy – the average constituency has 67,000 voters and so you face considerable competition for their time. However, they are generally more receptive to constituency lobbying than they have been in the past. They are also better staffed nowadays and appreciate that they need to campaign on various issues throughout their term in Parliament.

Keep in contact with your MP. They will have many campaigns, committees and constituency issues all running at the same time. Their staff can be busy so always offer as much information as you can about the campaign that you are running.

You need to be clear in your own mind what you want from your local elected representative and what they may be capable of delivering. Your local council is elected to make sure that local services (e.g. education, housing, planning and social services) are adequate; but your MP is elected to represent you at the national level. MPs will often have local councillors at their surgeries to help constituents whose problems are related to the provision of local services. However, if you know your problem relates to local services then the best place to start is your local council.

There is a wide range of actions that a sympathetic MP can undertake on your behalf, from speaking in public to making private enquiries to assist the campaign and even bringing your issue to public attention on the floor of the House of Commons. A supportive letter from your MP on House of Commons notepaper to the relevant company, department or official might be enough to draw attention to your concerns where previous attempts have failed. Equally, your MP may decide to raise the issue in the House of Commons, which would bring press and public attention.

There are a number of particular ways in which your MP can raise issues relating to your campaign in the House of Commons. The main ones are as follows:

- **Parliamentary questions.** You can ask your MP to put the relevant minister on the spot by asking them to pose a question.

MPs can ask the government questions to be answered in person by a minister (oral questions) or in writing (written questions). Oral questions are often used to attack (or support) government policy, but written questions better lend themselves to extracting more detailed information. Oral questions are a handy way for sympathetic MPs to bring a constituency issue to a minister's notice and are, consequently, very useful for campaigners. They generally have to be tabled at least three sitting days before the relevant session. Written questions are useful for extricating particular nuggets of information. In 2005/06 nearly 86,000 questions were tabled by MPs and 78,000 received responses: 17,000 for an oral answer and 61,000 for a written answer. According to the rules, a parliamentary question must either seek information (e.g. What? How many? When?) or press for action. A question must not 'offer or seek expressions of opinion' nor 'convey information or advance a proposition, an argument or debate'. In addition the question must have a factual base; in other words, it shouldn't seek confirmation of rumours in media reports.

To find out more check out fact sheet P1 at www.parliament. uk/documents/upload/p01.pdf.

- **Adjournment debates.** These are the half-hour adjournment periods at the end of the day. During this time an MP can speak on a subject of their choice. Your MP must apply to the Speaker (who chairs proceedings in the Commons) and a weekly ballot is held, and four MPs gain the right to speak during the following week and the Speaker chooses a fifth. Normally, only the MP raising the matter and the minister responsible for replying speak during an adjournment debate. It can put an issue on the government department's agenda and MPs will usually seek the support of other MPs in order to come along to the debate, therefore raising the profile around Parliament. Ministers replying to adjournment debates are often willing to have follow-up meetings with the MP and you will have the satisfaction of the issue you are raising being debated in the House of Commons.

- **Early Day Motions (EDMs).** These are a much-used weapon in the campaigner's armoury to raise awareness of an issue. It is a motion tabled by a MP for which no date has been fixed for a debate. They are almost never debated on the floor of the House of Commons – the main point is to form a kind of petition that MPs can sign demonstrating support for a given cause. They can range from the trivial, for example, MPs trying to win a bit of press on the back of the success of their local football team, through to the serious, such as calls for the impeachment of the then Prime Minister Tony Blair over the Iraq war. An EDM must begin with the words, 'That this house…' and must not exceed 250 words.

Although EDMs are rarely debated, it is possible for an MP to ask for them to be debated in 'Business questions' on a Thursday. Raising the EDM on the floor of the House of Commons can help generate press coverage especially in the local media. See chapter 6 for the Ban Foie Gras campaign, which encouraged campaigners to lobby their MPs online. To find out more check out fact sheet P1 on the Parliament website www.parliament.uk/documents/upload/p01.pdf.

'Early Day Motions (EDMs) can range from the slightly bizarre to heavyweight ones concerning what's going on in Iraq,' says Keith Vaz, the Labour MP for Leicester East and one of the most prolific users of the EDM in Westminster. He tabled 40 EDMs in one parliamentary session in 2007 (including, asking for recognition of Leicester's success in the Curry Capital of Britain awards and concerns over alleged racism towards a Bollywood star on the TV reality show *Big Brother*, which sparked a national debate).

Are EDMs effective? 'They are an important parliamentary tool for an MP to raise awareness on key issues such as legal aid reform or good charitable causes,' explains the MP. 'The one problem I have is explaining to people what an EDM is. I just say that "I'm raising the matter in Parliament".'

What is a good level of support for an EDM? He says the backing of 100 MPs makes it credible and one 'that should guarantee a debate' – but, of course, there are no guarantees.

What is the most useful thing an MP can do on behalf of a constituent wanting to start a campaign? 'I would start with asking them to write a letter to the minister and then consider tabling a parliamentary question,' he replies. 'Then consider an EDM, there is then the possibility of an adjournment debate and a Private Members' bill.'

- **Private Members' bills.** A sympathetic MP can introduce such a bill. There are three ways of introducing such bills. A ballot bill has the best chance of becoming law, as it gets priority for the limited amount of debating time available. The names of MPs applying for a bill are drawn in a ballot held at the beginning of the parliamentary year. Normally, the first seven ballot bills get a day's debate. Ten Minute Rule bills can be an opportunity for MPs to voice their concerns, rather than a serious attempt to get a bill passed. They make speeches of no more than ten minutes outlining their position, which another Member may oppose in a similar short statement. It is a good opportunity to raise the profile of an issue and to see whether it has support among other MPs. Any MP may introduce a presentation bill. They introduce the title but do not speak in support of it – they rarely become law.

The European Union

Structure

There are now 492 million people living in 27 member states which make up the European Union (EU). There are five main institutions:

1. **The European Parliament.** Where the real power to make European law lies. It is the only directly elected EU institution and has 785 members, elected by people in the individual member states. All European laws are passed by your MEP and your minister in the Council of Ministers. Parliament meets in Brussels and Strasbourg.

2. **Council of Ministers.** Comprises ministers from each member state with specific areas of responsibility; for example, environment ministers meet to pass laws on controlling pollution. The Council of Ministers meets in Brussels and Luxembourg.

3. **European Council.** Made up of the heads of state or government plus the President of the European Commission. It sets the overall agenda for EU policies and meets in Brussels four times a year.

4. **European Commission.** Proposes European laws and ensures that policies are enforced. The European Commissioners are appointed for a five-year term, one from each of the 27 member states. They swear to put the interests of the EU above the interests of their countries. The European Parliament monitors the Commission's activities and can bring a motion of censure to dismiss it. It is based in Brussels.

5. **The European Court of Justice.** Makes sure that countries comply with EU law and settles dispute over how treaties and legislation are interpreted. It is based in Luxembourg and is not to be confused with the European Court of Human Rights, which isn't part of the EU and is based in Strasbourg.

CASE STUDY: SURFERS AGAINST SEWAGE

'European legislation is a great driver for getting our beaches and seas cleaner,' says Andy Cummins, campaigns officer with Surfers Against Sewage (SAS).'We have worked hard lobbying on the new Bathing Water Directive for a number of years.The first directive came out in 1976 and 30 years on, the way we use the sea has changed dramatically and we needed the legislation to catch up and protect all recreational water users. We have been extremely successful with the new Bathing Water Directive, but there is still a huge amount to be done.'

SAS began their campaign in 1990 with the aim of cleaning up two beaches, St Agnes and Porthtowan; since then it has grown to a group with as many as 10,000 supporters.

Why are they campaigning? Andy Cummins says, 'Coming into contact with sewage while surfing, swimming, diving or any other recreational watersport isn't pleasant and can leave you seriously ill. For example, World Health Organisation [WHO] research shows that surfers are three times more likely to contract hepatitis A than the general public.'

SAS has been campaigning for better protection for recreational water users through the EU Bathing Water Directive that dates back to 1976. The legislation provides for the testing of water quality across the EU over a 20-week bathing season from the beginning of May to the end of September. Beaches are classified as excellent, good or poor. 'We argue that standards are completely out of sync with world health expert opinion; for example, a beach passing the 'good water' quality standard still presents a bather with a 12–15% risk of contracting gastroenteritis,' Cummins says.

What are they doing about it? SAS has campaigned for a revision of this Directive and their work has already paid off. An EU agreement made in 2006 will lead to improvements (starting in 2008), including a tightening of the water quality standards. 'We're disappointed that the new Directive failed to define "recreational water users" within the definition of "bather" because certain groups of recreational water users (such as surfers) are more at risk of falling sick than bathers,' he says. 'There is a small caveat in the new Directive that promises to investigate the impact on recreational water users, so the campaigning will go on. We were also disappointed that the Directive only relates to designated bathing waters and only accounts for water quality sampling in the bathing season.'

How does the group get MEPs involved? Cummins says, 'There is a lot of credible science and data coming from organisations such as the World Health Organisation [WHO]. We have the support of several sympathetic MEPs and because of our high media profile we can attract support from other less passionate MEPs. When there were MEP elections in the South-West we invited them all for surf lessons straight away, trying to get them all involved in the campaign and to sign up to our clean water manifesto. SAS aren't aligned with any one political party, so we invited MEPs from all the parties. This also improved the chances of having the press covering the event. MEPs work in a similar way to MPs and will respond to what is in the post. We encourage members to write to their MEPs on behalf of SAS. This is surprisingly successful without it taking thousands of letters to get the cause noticed. With the letter writing campaign we make sure that the MEPs are aware of the problems facing recreational water users in their constituency. Once we have done all this we make sure we are available for comment.'

What MEPs do

A sympathetic MEP might well be able to advance your cause in much the same way as an MP can – by creating debate and raising the profile of the issue in the media. Many campaigns also have a European angle – especially if that campaign relates to environmental protection or food safety standards where much of the legislation now on our statute books began in Europe.

MEPs have the power to approve, amend or reject EU legislation. The European Parliament and MEPs have been responsible for creating, for example, the Working Time Directive, which means that all workers – full-time, part-time and temporary – now enjoy the right to four weeks' paid holiday, shorter working hours and the maximum 48-hour working week rule (although the UK has an opt-out agreement). The European Parliament was also responsible for developing clear labelling on genetically modified food.

MEPs divide their working lives between their regional constituencies in the UK and the public committee meetings in Brussels. For one week in every month they go to Strasbourg where all MEPs come together in full session to debate and vote on legislation. Most of the 78 MEPs from the UK sit in multinational political groupings in the European Parliament alongside members from other countries with broadly similar views. They do much of their political work as members of at least one of 20 specialist policy committees which range from foreign affairs, civil liberties, justice and home affairs to environment, public health, food safety and international trade. Each region in the UK has between three and ten MEPs all of whom represent constituencies in the whole region.

For more information see www.europarl.org.uk (where you can find out who your MP is plus it includes the online leaflet *What Do Your MEPs Do?* in the publications section of this website).

CASE STUDY: RESIDENTS AGAINST RUBBISH

'Residents against Rubbish is a small group of concerned and like-minded people with one goal – to stop companies and councils treating our area as a dumping ground for waste'.

Why are they campaigning? 'People may think we're just moaning NIMBYs but that is not true. As a group we feel that dumping rubbish into the ground is a poor solution to our waste problems. As a group we want to prevent landfill at Pathhead, Ryton. We live in an area where there have already been a number of landfills, and we want to protect our environment.'

Why is Europe relevant to your campaign? 'We approached our local MEP Fiona Hall (the Liberal Democrat MEP for the North East) about petitioning the European Parliament. Any EU citizen may submit a petition "on a subject which comes within the European Union's fields of activity and which affects them directly". She gave us the forms and her admin staff gave guidance.

Our claim was declared admissible by the European Parliament's petitions' committee in November 2005. By this time, we knew that there was no possibility of legal proceedings making any difference in the UK so Europe became our main focus.

The case was first heard in committee in April 2006. Whilst the EC felt that the plans complied with regulations, they were overruled by the petitions' committee. One of our committee members, Daniel Grey, spoke on our behalf and Fiona Hall also expressed her concerns.

The second hearing was in October 2006. Daniel and Fiona again spoke and there was written support from local Labour and Conservative MEPs. Again, the Commissioners felt there was no breach of regulations but, once these submissions had been made, a unanimous decision was taken to keep the case open and request more detailed information from the council, the Environment Agency and the waste company SITA.

A further meeting was held in Brussels in September 2007. Daniel again presented our case, and there was a unanimous decision in our favour. This time the European Commissioners expressed grave concerns about the groundwater issue as well as the environmental impact.'

What happens next? 'The Commissioners asked for information from the Environment Agency as a matter of urgency and plan to write to the UK authorities requesting suspension of landfilling operations during the inquiries. The Commissioners can rule that the UK is in breach of its duties under the directives on landfill and groundwater. This means that the authorities will be forced to do something about Pathhead and all other sites in a similar position. This is what we've been hoping for since we started this campaign.'

What did it cost? 'It cost about £1,000 for each trip to Brussels. In order to present our case, we needed detailed documentation, photographic evidence and, of course, the expertise of Daniel and Fiona.'

CHAPTER 6

Going online

> 'It's just me, the website with some video clips and an email list. That's all you need… This kind of "guerrilla" campaigning is different because we are campaigning on the Internet.'
>
> Paul Blanchard, Ban Foie Gras campaign

Having an online presence is a must for most campaigns these days. For the computer novice, you should be reassured because you can get started without any specialist technological knowledge and without spending much, if any, money. This chapter covers the services, software and techniques that you can use to have an effective online campaign – all of which can cost you nothing.

There is no one way to have a Web presence. The blogging phenomenon is one of the clearest manifestations of 'people power' in recent years. A blog is an online journal or diary which is a means to share information and ideas. Blogs have been made widely available by free, easy-to-use sites that will host it for you. For those campaigners who are more comfortable in cyberspace and for those willing to have a go, then social networking sites, such as Facebook and MySpace, as well as photo and video sharing sites like Flickr and YouTube, can become essential components of your campaign.

A few years ago, it would have been an expensive business to reach millions of people with your thoughts online. Now not only can you do that at no expense, but you can enable Web-users to see your campaign photos, check out video footage, listen to sound files, as well as provide discussion forums and online networks for your supporters and anyone wanting to join the debate. In the recent past, you would have had to hire a Web designer to build you a site. There would have been an expense for that input as well as costs for storage capacity for the video and audio files (not to mention the discussion forum software and a database). Not any more. You can do it all for free and do it immediately. The group could consider appointing a dedicated website or IT officer who can be responsible for the running and updating of the site or blog. If you have a member who is IT literate, they might well be a good candidate for the position.

The Internet is constantly evolving, which means that the technology, software and services quickly become outdated. However, with that in mind, this chapter will show you how to use free services and sites to get your campaign messages online, get them noticed and to meet other campaigners working on similar issues.

CASE STUDY: BAN FOIE GRAS – CONTACT BLANCHARD

Paul Blanchard is a Labour councillor in York who is trying to outlaw the sale of foie gras (www.banfoiegras.org.uk). He calls it a 'guerrilla campaign'. 'It's just me, the website with some video clips and an email list. That's all you need,' he says. The group has 11,000 people on his email list.

The campaign in its first year scored a number of notable successes – York City Council became the first council in the UK to pass a motion condemning the sale of the controversial food product anywhere in the city; 138 MPs signed up to an Early Day Motion (EDM) calling for an outright ban; and 9,000 people have signed a petition on the Downing Street website. Foie gras is produced by force-feeding ducks and geese until their livers become enlarged. 'It is so cruel it is banned in 15 countries,' Blanchard told the press. 'I believe York can play its part to get foie gras banned in the UK. Production is already banned in Britain on cruelty grounds, but because the sale is still allowed, we are still one of the biggest importers of foie gras from France.'

How much does it cost to run an online campaign? Not as much as you think, Blanchard replies. 'It is more a question of the time it takes. The domain name and the Internet hosting cost about £50. The website uses a 'content management system', and an animal welfare enthusiast has offered to look after that for free. I don't use automated email management software. I just send an email from Microsoft Outlook, blind carbon copied (i.e. sent to multiple recipients without disclosing the email addresses of other recipients) to 11,000 people. It's time-consuming but in terms of money it hasn't cost much at all – less than £100. This kind of guerrilla campaigning is different because we are campaigning on the Internet. It is a question of using both old and new media. You need to have the momentum which is "old media" led. You need to be in the papers, on *Channel 4 News* and on *Sky News* to generate the Internet interest and that creates a momentum that perpetuates itself. The most time-consuming part has been dealing with letters of support. If someone emails you the equivalent of two sides of A4 about why they support you it appears rude to send a generic response.'

One of the most effective aspects of the online campaign has been persuading MPs to sign up to the Early Day Motion supporting a ban, by an online automated form through an external site www.vote4animals.org.uk. 'You enter your postcode and it works out who your MP is and then you automatically send them an email from the site. We probably persuaded about 50 MPs to support it because it was so easy. A constituent could lobby their MP from start to finish in about 60 seconds.'

Campaigning online

The Internet has changed. A few years ago it was seen as an online version of TV. Websites were the medium to deliver content to passive receivers and the communication was one-way. Now the Web is about having conversations and sites offer ways for us to leave comments and join debates. BBC Online encourages people to send in their pictures; many newspapers encourage readers to post comments on their articles, and discuss and debate issues; Amazon allows its customers to review and recommend books, creating a network of groups, forums, discussion boards and networks, so users of a product can discuss it, offer tips and solve problems.

A key thing to understand about the Internet, particularly when it comes to campaigning, is that it is an increasingly 'open source'. The term comes from computer programming where a programmer creates software, uploads it to the Internet enabling anyone access to add to it, change it and make it better. The same idea now applies to information. Wikipedia is an online encyclopaedia where anyone can add new material or edit existing entries and make them better. Some argue that this encyclopaedia built from the bottom-up is as accurate and comprehensive as traditional paper encyclopaedias. The most popular sites, such as YouTube and Facebook, work because thousands of people are adding material and linking their stories together into communities of interest around a particular band, brand or issue.

'The Web is a great place to tell stories and a campaign is a form of story,' says Paul Caplan, who runs the Internationale (www.theinternationale.org), a company that helps charities and government exploit the benefits of what he calls the 'Live Web'. 'The

Live Web is like a party. There are two ways of meeting people at a party. One, you stand in the corner of the room and shout "I am a very interesting person. I have important things to say. Gather round…" You're probably not going to get very far with that approach. The other way of meeting people at a party is to circulate and listen. You're in one group chatting about something and you chip in, "That's interesting, I remember when…" Then you move on to another group and add your little bit. You network and join in conversations.'

The analogy with the Web is that there are blogs and sites that stand in a corner shouting out their message, but the ones that are interesting are the ones where stories start conversations or spring from other conversations. 'The Web offers you the world's biggest party at which to tell your campaign story. Your story is just the starting point because other people will add their comments, their ideas and their stories – just like they do in a conversation at a party. That is why it is so powerful,' Paul Caplan argues. 'The Web offers you the world's biggest party. Conversations lead to connections which lead to ideas which lead to relationships which make for effective and creative campaigning.' This chapter has been written with the help of Paul Caplan.

Blogging

A blog is a regularly updated Web page where the entries are arranged with the most recent at the top. Entries can be short or long. They can be well-considered or just dashed off in a moment of inspiration. The best are very personal and passionate.

The 'blogosphere' has established itself as the domain of the campaigner (as well as that of celebrity gossip mongers and anyone who thinks, rightly or wrongly, that they have something to say). It's also a crowded place – one estimate reckons as many as four million bloggers are at work in the UK (The *Guardian*, November 2007).

Nonetheless, online campaigns can be hugely effective. Consider

Laurie Pycroft, a 16-year-old who founded a pro-animal testing campaign which managed to redefine the terms of the vivisection debate. The campaign Pro-Test (www.Pro-Test.org.uk) was primarily run from his bedroom and operated through his blog (see case study). A month later, he led a march of 1,000 demonstrators through Oxford calling for the right to conduct medical research on animals and the campaign now has the support of eminent scientists such as Robert Winston and the neurosurgeon Tipu Aziz.

'The Internet has played an important part in the campaign,' says Tom Holder of Pro-Test. It was Laurie Pycroft, a 16-year-old, who founded the pro-vivisection campaign. 'Whilst Laurie was doing his own thing, I started a blog on the social networking site Facebook saying, in jest, that animal rights activists were driving me so mad that it made me want to kill small furry animals,' says Holder, a graduate from Cambridge. 'It was a little joke but 50 people every day were joining.' Facebook quickly shut down the blog, but by that time Holder had some support. 'I was operating independently from Laurie, but as soon as he said that he was going to organise a march I contacted him through the website and suggested that he needed students to help.' One month after the website (www.Pro-Test.org.uk) was launched in 2006, about one thousand people came out to march in support of Pro-Test (whereas animal rights activists persuaded only 150 to come out on the same day).

Another high-profile example is Jeff Jarvis, who reported his bad experiences at the hands of the computer giant Dell's customer service staff via his blog (www.buzzmachine.com). The phrase 'Dell Hell' was coined and fellow shoppers joined in with horror stories about the company. The bad publicity spread like wildfire online and was picked up by the search engines with 10 million references to 'Dell Hell' on Google. Suddenly consumers searching to buy Dell products were being presented with search results that included very unfavourable blog posts. Online concerns quickly transferred to the conventional press worldwide. In the end Dell changed its customer service policy.

CASE STUDY: PRO-TEST

Why is an online campaign effective? 'There are three main elements of our Web presence – the website, the blog (called "Standing up for science") and the social networking sites (mainly Facebook),' explains Pro-Test's Tom Holder. 'A website is really easy to tell your friends about. It clearly states what your aims and goals are. Everyone can see it, everyone knows what they're getting involved with, and they can decide from there if they want to get further involved. A blog is good way of telling people how the campaign is going and what progress you are making. Don't underestimate the social networking sites, especially if your campaign is directed towards young people. People find it a lot easier from there to find your website – plus, they can see what groups their friends are joining, and that gives a site a bit of momentum. A Web presence can grow very quickly.'

It doesn't take much effort to show support in cyberspace, not like turning up to a demo. Does online support count? 'We find that passive support is really important. We are about changing attitudes and people who have shown passive support have demonstrated that they go along with the attitudes that we have even though they might not be willing to be actively involved. We measure success not just by polls, but by how our Facebook group is going. We now have 2,500 people on it which has been fantastic.'

What's the advantage of Facebook? 'It means that we can contact supporters. Secondly, it offers a forum for debate because Facebook has a message board. We have people of the opposing view trying to argue and so it is good for finding out what arguments are persuasive. We've found it important to know what pseudoscience is used by the other side so that we can debunk it. What we have found is that people don't know how to respond when they are faced with the kind of facts that we have at our disposal. A lot of teenagers take part in arguments on the message boards and we've been able to give them the information so that they can win the little arguments that they have on these message boards.'

How much does it cost to maintain an online presence? 'It is a remarkably small amount. We pay a website administrator £50 a month. Webspace is becoming very cheap.'

So why blog? For someone with something to say but little technical skill, a blog provides the cheapest and easiest way to have an Internet presence. Unlike building a website, you don't have to write your own HTML (the language of Web pages) nor do you need design skills. The low-fi option is simply to use a hosted blogging platform which can be easily customised by selecting a design from the available templates and adding the content and functions that you want. From registering to publishing your first post, can take as little as five minutes.

One of the big advantages of this way, as opposed to running your own website, is that your blog sits on the provider's server – so not only will you spend nothing on designing and developing a site, but you won't need to pay any hosting costs either. All you need is a computer, a connection to the Internet and the enthusiasm to write and publish compelling content on a regular basis.

Three of the biggest and most mainstream blogging platforms are wordpress.com, blogger.com and typepad.com.

The best way to understand blogging is to blog. To get started, go to the website www.wordpress.com and click on the 'Sign Up Now' button. After a few clicks you'll be up and running. Think about what to call your blog. If you create one at Wordpress, your blog's Web address will be 'username.wordpress.com' (e.g. to use a fictional example, www.saveourturtles.wordpress.com). So you might want to think about what username to use. You could use your group's name, or your 'issue'. Remember, though, the longer it is the more your reader will have to type.

To the outside world there will be little difference between your blog page and a website other than your URL (website address) which will incorporate the blog name. For the purposes of publicising your campaign it might be worthwhile selecting a snappy name that captures the public's imagination and then trying to register that name as either a domain name or an Internet address (e.g. www.saveourturtles.com), if it is available. Once bought, this can then be used instead of the longer original. All your campaign literature, posters and t-shirts could be branded with this Web address. You can find out within minutes if your domain name of choice is available by visiting a domain name registration site. These are easily found by Googling 'domain names'. There are hundreds of UK-based traders from which to buy a name – shop around to get the best price because it will vary. While sought-after domain names command huge fees, you could get yours for as little as £5 per year. If you need further guidance, then Nominet, the company that registers all UK domain names, offers advice on how to register on its website at www.nominet.org.uk. Once you've bought a suitable domain name you can tell the company you bought it from to redirect visitors to your blog (or 'repoint' it).

If you already have a website, simply add a link to 'my blog' on your Web page. If you're feeling adventurous you can install the free Wordpress blog software on your own site. Go to www.wordpress.org and follow the instructions. You might even consider having more than one blog across your campaign group.

TOP TIPS

In terms of style, let your passion and enthusiasm shine through, advises Paul Caplan.

Sometimes there might be spelling mistakes; sometimes your grammar might make your old English teacher grimace. It doesn't matter. Concentrate on your passion, enthusiasm and ideas. That's what's going to get people reading and want to start conversations, connections and relationships.

Your aim should be to get people talking to you. Ask them questions, link to their blogs, comment on the news or latest developments. Tell real stories and ask for responses and other stories. Invite people to join in and talk to you as you would in a real-life conversation.

Think of using sentences such as:

- 'At least that's how I see it. What do you think?'
- 'If you've got any other examples, let me know.'
- 'I don't know. Anyone got any ideas?'

Find out how other blogs cover similar issues. Go to the blog search site www.technorati.com and do a search for your issue (as well as on YouTube and Flickr for video and photographs). If you find a blog on your issue, you could write a blog in response, linking to the original story; for example, 'I read on such and such a blog that… but I think that…' Your blog will automatically post your response as a comment on the original author's blog. Where you take that relationship next is up to you. Perhaps you carry on talking to your fellow blogger. Perhaps you see if there's a campaign or fundraising initiative you can work on together. Perhaps you get a new perspective or idea.

Your blog stories will automatically be picked up by the Technorati website, but you can help people find your stories by adding 'keywords' or 'tags' to each story. Again, that is explained on the Wordpress site. Blogging is the most accessible way to join the online party. It's just writing – if you can remember how to talk like a human being, you're away.

Pictures

The London Marathon is a massive event in the charity calendar and an opportunity for a group to raise its profile. Many charities and charity supporters take part in the event to raise money and awareness. Photographs of the Marathon are very popular (do a search on a photo-sharing site such as Flickr (www.flickr.com)). You could pay a professional photographer to get pictures of your supporters crossing the finish line, but there is another, cheaper and more effective way.

It is likely that every runner will have their family to support them and they will all have cameras (or mobile phones) with them and they'll be taking pictures of their loved ones falling over the finish line. The chances are that any children will already post the embarrassing pictures of their exhausted parents to their blogs and social network sites like Facebook and MySpace. They may also be uploading them to Flickr. As with blog postings, people can 'tag' their photos by using keywords. You could ask all of your runners' families to use the same tags, such as 'London Marathon' and your charity name. This links all the photos on blogs, Flickr, etc together when anyone searches on the Technorati website.

So someone searching for pictures of the London Marathon would find your pictures and then click on your tag and be shown all the other pictures tagged with your group's name – maybe more fundraising pictures, maybe some of your work, some taken by you, some by your supporters or service users. Then that person searching the Internet would have a virtual introduction to you and your work and may leave a comment on your pictures or go on to read your blog or become a new supporter.

This can work the other way round as well. Go on to Flickr and search for a tag that's relevant to the campaign. You'll find thousands of people around the world taking pictures and tagging them with words relevant to your campaign (e.g. disability, cancer, pollution). You may find a photographer who is passionate about the same things you are. So leave them a comment (e.g. 'I found your photo. I work for a small campaigning group in...that helps old people. I'd be interested in hearing about your project. Maybe there's a way we could work together...).'

A few years ago if you'd wanted to have photos on your website, as a gallery or for supporters or the media to download images, you'd have had to pay a computer programmer and a Web designer to create new pages, but not now. You can do this for free through the Flickr site. Create your account, upload some photos with their tags, and then Flickr will give you a simple piece of computer code that you can put on your Web page or even your blog – Wordpress makes it very easy with a plug-in. When a visitor clicks on the link, they get taken to your Flickr page where they get introduced to your photos to get an idea of the sort of things you do.

Video

The website YouTube does the same job for videos as Flickr does for photos. You upload a video, tag it and people can search for it, comment on your work and start conversations. You can find others making films in your area and you can embed a video in your site (in other words it plays on your website). There are no hosting costs, no bandwidth issues and no headaches for your IT person. You can even embed them on your blog hosted on Wordpress.

CASE STUDY: GENERATION WHY

Ben Beaumont, editor of Oxfam's Generation Why website, argues that blogging is a great way to keep supporters updated on campaigns, especially when used in conjunction with social networking tools like Facebook or MySpace (see MySpace.com/starbucksaction for an example).

'I use TakingItGlobal (www.takingitglobal.org) as you can create your blog and also share it with people all over the world,' says Oxfam campaigner Sara Darr. 'As a result, you're able to network, meet new friends, develop your writing skills and share your experiences.'

Obviously, it's unlikely (unless you hit upon something truly unique) that your blog will be read by millions, but it can still be a great place to start your campaigning. At the very least, it will help you formulate your arguments and sharpen your writing skills. If you make sure you plug it to family, friends and campaign contacts – and encourage them to add comments and feedback – it can be the best place to share news, events and other interesting campaign snippets.

Your blog will also be a great way to tell people about different campaign actions, and start the debate about the issues. If you publicise your blog in the right ways, you'll be able to hook up with people blogging about similar issues, and start a whole chain of people linking to each other. And it may even get noticed by the national media.

'It is no surprise that virtually all national online newspapers use bloggers to gather reports and opinion from around the globe,' says another Oxfam campaigner, Rhodri Davies. 'Other outlets have got on the case as well – CNN was said to be using UK bloggers as information sources on 7/7 and stockbrokers even use blogs to discover opinions on new products whose manufacturers they may invest in.'

An important tip for bloggers is – keep going. Blogs need to be updated regularly.

If you're worried about the amount of time keeping up with reading other bloggers and joining in the conversation will take, set yourself some limits. Set aside half an hour a week. Subscribe to some blogs that are relevant (you can use a site like bloglines.com to make that easy), leave a couple of comments and write something on your blog. Make it clear to your readers that you only update the blog every Friday or whatever.

Then, after a few weeks, take a look. Have you found any new contacts or information? Have you generated any interest? Has anyone subscribed to your blog (you can use www.feedburner.com to check)? Have any journalists been in touch? If things have started to move you might want to look at the amount of time you spend doing traditional 'publicity'.

So, if you're feeling inspired, angry or frustrated by the world around you, why not start a blog? It's as easy as pie, and you might just make a difference.

CHAPTER 7

Information

> 'As the saying goes – the cost of freedom is eternal vigilance. Asking questions of our public bodies is the best way to ensure they are working for our interests and not those of politicians.'
>
> Heather Brooke, freedom of information campaigner

You know what your own objectives are but you need to make a compelling case as well. Your campaign must have depth and it must be supported by a comprehensive and well-researched information base. Effective campaigns are built on good research. If, as a campaigner, you are holding yourself out as an authority on a subject, then you have a serious responsibility to ensure that you and your office holders are well-briefed and a source of reliable information. You need to be regarded as such by journalists, politicians, prospective funders and even – perhaps, especially – by your opponents, in order to be a credible voice in the debate. This means that you should have a firm grip on all the available information, not just when it furthers your cause. The consequences of burying your head in the sand about the existence of counter-arguments are dire. You don't want to be caught out mid-debate. Forewarned is forearmed.

Potential funders and donors will expect your message to be grounded in the best available research before committing any money.

Obtaining good quality research does not mean spending huge sums commissioning professional analysts, but it does require a methodical approach to ensure that any findings you rely on will stand up to scrutiny by your opponents.

Obtaining information and documentation has been made easier in recent years by the introduction of legislation promoting 'open government'. This means (in theory, at least) that government is clear, transparent and subject to scrutiny about the information it holds. The availability of information on the Internet does mean that much more is readily accessible (e.g. planning applications and related documents on local government websites). Also, public bodies such as local councils and health authorities are starting to recognise their freedom of information obligations (much of which only became law in 2005), although this can be a bit hit-and-miss.

'Since the new "right to know" laws came into force in January 2005 campaigners have had a new and powerful tool in their toolbox,' says Phil Michaels, head of legal at Friends of the Earth's rights and justice centre. 'Information is the key to every successful campaign and this legislation means that we can now access information that would never previously have seen the light of day. Persistence and a bit of basic legal knowledge will go a very long way.'

It is important to appreciate that the concept of 'open government' is selective, and it may well be that the organisation holding the information you want will – quite possibly unlawfully – be unwilling to give it up. You therefore need to know your rights to access the information and how to best obtain it.

CHAPTER OVERVIEW:

- Compiling your evidence base
- Conducting your own research
- Your right to information

Compiling your evidence base

An effective campaign is a well-researched campaign. You may be experts in your field and it is your experience working on the issues involved that gives you legitimacy. However, the quality of your evidence is critically important if you want to demonstrate your credibility in the debate. 'Experts' findings can't easily be dismissed,' says Louise Barton, chair of the Lydd Airport Action Group (LAAG). 'If we say something as amateurs, we can be dismissed, but expert opinion carries weight and it is surprisingly affordable. Rather than spending all our hard-raised funds on PR, demos and leaflets, we've spent some of the money on expert opinion and so far it's paying off.' See case study below.

CASE STUDY: LAAG

LAAG was formed by local people living on Romney Marsh in Kent to prevent the expansion of their small local airport into a major regional airport capable of handling up to two million passengers a year. The airport is enclosed by the Dungeness, Romney Marsh and Rye Bay Site of Special Scientific Interest, and is next to the RSPB's oldest bird reserve and three miles from Dungeness nuclear power station. The campaign is ongoing. Louise Barton explains why expert evidence has made a difference to their campaign.

'We were able to demonstrate local support. Backers of the airport scheme claimed local people supported expansion. But that was proved false by using the provisions of the Local Government Act, Part III, to obtain a parish referendum where the expansion plans were overwhelmingly rejected. Referendums are surprisingly easy to organise, but it is important to make sure the procedures are followed accurately otherwise councils can stop them.'

Basic principles

Good quality evidence needs to be:

- **Robust.** Check all your evidence thoroughly. Be truthful and do not exaggerate details to make a case. The opposition as well as others (such as potential allies, prospective funders, or government departments) are likely to have greater resources than you and they might well deploy advisers to go through your evidence with a fine toothcomb. Ensure that your sources are reliable and back up claims with expert opinion wherever possible. When using research, especially from external sources, be sure that you know how it was conducted and what methodology was used. Also take care not to use research selectively and to your advantage, thus misrepresenting the findings as a whole. Apart from anything else, you will be found out.

- **Objective.** You need to be credible and not to lay yourself open to criticism that your attempts to compile evidence are merely self-serving.

- **Relevant.** Stick to the issue and be as focused as possible. Do not overwhelm recipients, but narrow down your evidence to points of concern and try to make sure that it is tailored towards the requirements of those recipients. If it can be packaged to fit their particular needs, it is more likely to be taken seriously.

- **Practical.** Offer realistic alternatives wherever possible. It is not enough to bemoan the state of the world – try to find precedents for any proposed solutions. Where has it been done before? What were the results? What benefits could it offer? Or what damage will be done if this course of action is not followed?

- **Compelling.** Real-life experiences can be powerful and persuasive, especially if combined with well-researched facts.

- **Well-presented.** Find out how various organisations like to receive information. Package the evidence accordingly and make sure that any reports include a summary, references (with sources for data) and your group's recommendations if appropriate. You must also make sure you date the evidence.

Conducting your own research

Research might seem straightforward. You ask people a number of questions and obtain the information you need. However, no matter how valid your attempts are to demonstrate the scale of the perceived problem, your detractors can quickly undermine you by seizing on any failings in your analysis to score points against you. On the other hand commissioning your own market research might well seem an expense that you cannot justify, but there is nothing to stop you conducting your own survey and there are other ways to reduce costs.

Research depends upon the co-operation of the public; people give up their time to be interviewed and provide information about what they do and what they like. To this end the trade body, the Market Research Society (MRS), has a code of conduct (as well as its *Newcomers' Guide to Market and Social Research*). The key principle (what the MRS calls 'the foundation') is that nobody who provides information should be misled about what they are involved in. If it is a confidential survey, then there should be no follow-up sales calls, for example.

'The problem for campaigning organisations, not just the local ones but the big ones as well, is that they carry their agenda into the questions that they ask people to the degree it distorts their research and their interpretation of it,' says a leading market researcher. 'It's very understandable because most campaigning organisations are on the side of the angels. The point is that it undermines their work if they have not been objective.'

There are two basic types of research. The first is quantitative research, which you need to undertake if you want to be able to say that '23% of people said "Yes" ' or 'a quarter of the population' agree with such a proposition. In other words it generates 'hard', numerical data. Then there is qualitative research if you do not want numbers but need a particular sort of understanding; for example, you might want to know not only what people do but why they do it (what drives them, what they care about), or not simply what they want but why they want it (what needs it would meet, what comfort it would bring).

- **Quantitative research.** The classic image of the market researcher is the person standing on the street corner, clipboard in hand, interviewing passers-by. It is not the most common form of data collection; however, it does make the point about one of the key elements of research – that research is collecting information by talking to a relatively small number of people as representative of the views of a larger number. However, the MRS points out that it only works if you:

  - talk to the right number of people;

  - talk to the right type of people;

  - ask the right questions; and

  - analyse the data you get in the right way.

  It is easy to see the sense in this. If, for example, a car manufacturer wants to know how the public are likely to feel about its latest model, it is not enough to talk only to men. Women buy cars, and children also have a say and so they should be consulted too. It is not enough to simply talk to people who have bought other models of the manufacturers' cars; you need to speak to potential as well as current purchasers. The same considerations apply to campaign groups. If you are concerned about a dangerous crossing outside your child's school, don't just talk to parents around the school gate. What do the teachers think? What about other locals? What about the motorists? See the case study, 'Doing your own research'.

  How do you get the information that you need? There are two main methods – talking to people, either in person or over the phone, or sending out questionnaires through the post or by email.

People who take part in a quantitative survey are asked the same questions in the same order so that the information can be added together at the end to give an overall picture. It used to be that people would be contacted via 'random' sampling techniques. The names of potential respondents would be selected at random, for example, taking every 10th or 20th name from a list of all relevant names. The names could be taken from the electoral register. This is a relatively expensive approach to research and now most surveys are done by using quota methods. Quota sampling involves interviewing certain types of people and if the people whose views you need, for example, are men and women under 50 years old, and all have children under-11 years, then the interviewers will be asked to find and interview people of the same type. This generates a cross-section of all the people that you're interested in.

- **Qualitative research.** As mentioned before, this means finding out not simply what people do but why they do it; for example, what it is people like, or dislike, about a new development in the middle of your town or the quality of food served to your children at school. Why do people feel that way and what would they prefer? You tend to talk to fewer people in qualitative research work because it involves exploratory discussions rather than everybody being asked the same question.

  Research of this sort is almost invariably done face-to-face. One of the best-known techniques is to engage a focus group where a small group of relevant people are brought together for an hour or so to discuss an issue.

You might consider that you need professional input. The Market Research Society has a buyer's guide on its website, www.mrs.org.uk, which includes a directory. Before you contact any agencies you might want to consider what specific services you are looking for. Are you looking for advice only? Do you already have the data and need it analysed? If it is a full research project, will you expect a detailed report at the end or will you just need the findings to make your own assessment? Report writing costs money, and so you might want to do that work yourself.

It is a good idea to draft a research brief. The more information you can give an agency the more it is likely to provide a useful response. A brief should include:

- a summary of the background to the research;
- an outline of the opportunities or problems that need to be explored and details of what you want to do with the information;
- a description of those people whose views are of interest;
- an outline of questions that need answering (agencies will have their own views on proposed questions);
- suggestions as to how the data might be collected;
- a description of what you are expecting – advice only, data or full report; and
- timing (when do you need the agency's proposals and when is the information needed).

The cost of market research varies. One campaign group was offered £500 per question from one agency and £1,000 per question from MORI for a survey of 1,000 people.

For more information, see the Market Research Society's website (www.mrs.org.uk).

DOING YOUR OWN RESEARCH

'To be able to say that this data is useful, you need to be sure what you have is a valid representation of the views of the key people. This means that you have to talk to a cross-section of the relevant people, ask the right questions and be objective as possible.'

A leading market researcher advises campaigners on DIY market research.

Who are the relevant people? 'If it is a matter of local concern, then it will clearly be local residents. But you cannot talk to everybody, that's why research is research. Ask yourself questions. If it is a campaign for a road crossing outside a school, you should certainly talk to a cross-section of parents and teachers in and around the school, but you might also need to talk to people perhaps from every tenth house in the relevant streets. Ensure that you're getting a cross-section of the right people. If you interview only at the school, you won't speak to the disabled or the mums who are stuck indoors with the toddlers. In some cases you will need to suggest some interviews are done in the evenings and at weekends as well, because there are some people who aren't around during the day.'

What about asking the right questions? 'Be sure that the questions that you want to ask are comprehensive and comprehensible. Don't ask leading questions (for example, do not ask, "Do you think the arrival of an incinerator at the end of your road is going to…make your life worse, make you leave the area or have a catastrophic impact on the environment?"). It is just possible that other than you and your fellow campaigners, no-one cares.'

How many people should you talk to? 'If it is a local campaign and you are objecting to plans for a local incinerator, for example, then 250 people from the key area is a respectable figure. The magic number for national polls is usually 1,000 though this can, of course, be costly and may not be necessary. The main reason for a thousand or more is not the total figure itself but the subsets, the different groups within the total that you can then look at separately; for example, men and women might think differently on a subject, those with children have far stronger views than those without, or the elderly might disagree with younger people.'

Your right to information

The Freedom of Information Act 2000 (FOIA) came into force at the beginning of 2005, and has quickly become a useful weapon in the armoury of campaigners. When New Labour introduced the bill in Parliament, the then Home Secretary Jack Straw promised that it would 'transform the default setting from "this should be kept quiet unless…" to "this should be published unless…"' Some 100,000 public authorities are subject to the Act, including government departments, local authorities, schools, colleges, publicly owned companies and Parliament itself, but not the security and intelligence services or the courts.

Soon after the introduction of the FOIA, the Campaign for Freedom of Information published its guide to the new legislation, which explained that the Act gives you 'a wide-ranging right to see all kinds of information held by the government and public authorities'. The guide states that 'you can use the Act to find out about a problem affecting your community and to check whether an authority is doing enough to deal with it; to see how effective a policy has been; to find out about the authority's spending; to check whether an authority is doing what it says it is and to learn more about the real reasons for decisions'. Authorities can only withhold information if an exemption under the legislation allows them to. 'Even exempt information may have to be disclosed in the public interest', the guide continues. If you think information has been improperly withheld, then you can complain to the Information Commissioner, who can order that the information be made available.

Then there are the Environmental Information Regulations 2004 (EIR), which provide rights to information about pollution, conservation, food contamination and all other aspects of the environment. The main reason for distinguishing between environmental and other information is that the government has had to comply separately with EU environmental obligations requiring a more stringent regime. The process of applying for information and challenging refusals is broadly the same under the two regimes.

Finally, the Data Protection Act 1998 gives an individual the right to know what information is held about them and sets out rules to make sure that this information is handled properly. (The Data Protection Act is also relevant to campaigning if you or your group is holding information, as discussed in chapter 3.) This legislation was given a boost by the introduction of the FOIA and as a consequence your right to see information held about you has been strengthened.

So are our new rights to information easy to invoke? The new laws have proved useful and easy to use. 'The complexity of the legislation is really only a problem for the public authority,' Maurice Frankel, director of the Campaign for Freedom of Information, has said. 'All you have to do is write to the authority, or email them, and describe the information you want. You don't even have to cite the legislation, there's no set application form and there's no specific person you have to apply to. From the public's point of view, it couldn't be simpler.'

CASE STUDY: GULLIVERS ACTION GROUP

Anne-Marie Loader is from Gullivers Action Group in Bexhill-on-Sea, a group protesting against plans to build over 40 homes on a local bowling green. She had to make numerous attempts to persuade Rother District Council to show her the planning file before she succeeded.

'At first, the council's officers said, "You can't see the file; it contains confidential information which is not available to the public". Then they said that the planning officer was working on the file and so I couldn't inspect it. There was then the excuse that the council would have to remove some of the documents from the file before I could see it. Then I was told that the council offices closed at 4 pm and that I would not have enough time to look through the papers in an hour as there were far too many – why didn't I just look online instead? I did look online and discovered that the council had been selective in which documents it had made available. Of the documents that were on its website, many were blank, unreadable, duplicated or wrongly indexed.

> The planning file was in the public domain. Provided that I contacted them in advance, it should have been made available. You end up thinking that there is something in the file to hide. And, in our case, there certainly was – a report commissioned by the council which was critical of the development and something neither the council nor the developer wanted to be in the public domain.'

Who can you apply to?

The requirements under both the FOIA and the EIR relate only to 'public authorities' – this means, government departments or any organisation carrying out a public function (this latter category encompasses private organisations, such as a limited company, or even an individual, provided they are carrying on a public function).

The FOIA covers government departments, local authorities, NHS bodies including GPs, schools and colleges, the police, quangos, publicly funded companies, the BBC and Channel 4. Most organisations are listed in the FOIA schedule and that list is updated and online at www.foi.gov.uk.

Courts, tribunals and the security and intelligence services are not covered.

The EIR defines 'public authority' as those bodies listed under the FOIA plus 'any other body or other person that carries out functions of public administration; or any other body or person that has public responsibilities relating to the environment, exercises functions of a public nature relating to the environment; or provides public services relating to the environment'. According to the Campaign for Freedom of Information this could include 'private contractors providing environmental services, consultancy or research for public bodies' as well as utility companies. The EIR also covers the courts and intelligence services.

It will usually be clear whether or not the organisation is caught by the rules (and you can always check on www.foi.gov.uk, as said before). If you are dealing with a local council, an education authority or government department, or if the organisation is carrying out public functions, it will be covered. Under the law, organisations are required to have a publication scheme describing the type of information it publishes, is likely to publish, and whether it charges for it. You can check the organisation's website or ask for a hard copy. It could be possible that an organisation replies to a request for information by stating that it does not hold the information, even though it is of a public nature. If so, it should tell you who holds the information and either transfer your request or supply you with the correct contact details.

What authorities have to disclose

Campaigners were very critical of freedom of information legislation as it went through Parliament, claiming that the rights being offered were being diluted by a fairly comprehensive list of exemptions. At the time of going to press, the government is considering restricting further the rights of access to information held by ministers and MPs.

The present position is that public authorities can withhold information under the freedom of information regime if that disclosure would prejudice defence, international relations, law enforcement, commercial interests, the economy and collective cabinet responsibility, or inhibit frank discussions by officials. You should bear in mind that any exemptions are subject to a public interest test and information will have to be released if the public interest in disclosure is greater than the public interest in confidentiality. The starting point is that all information should be made available on request. It is for the authority to justify why it is unwilling to release information rather than your having to explain why the information should be released.

Making your request for information

Preparing an information request

You want your request to be as effective as possible and the following section offers you some pointers. In Appendix 5 there are model letters for applying for different types of information.

- **Put your request in writing.** An environmental information request can be as informal as picking up the telephone and making a call; but a request under the FOIA must be in writing by either letter or email. As a matter of good practice you should make all requests in writing. You will then have a record of when the request was made, who it was sent to and when it was sent. Address the request to the organisation's FOI officer.

- **Provide detail.** Try to make it as easy as possible for the person dealing with the request to locate the information. Provide all the appropriate references, dates and references to reports.

- **Be specific.** If, for example, the information request is to a council's environmental health department and relates to the way it has dealt with pollution from a local factory, the response could amount to hundreds of pages of reports. If so, the council could refuse to comply on the grounds of cost (see later). Pre-empt this by being clear as to what information is really going to help your case. Is there any point in obtaining information about matters ten years old, when the problems really only relate to the last few years?

  If you are only really interested in how the council has responded to local residents' complaints, you could phrase your request in the following way: 'Please provide a copy of all correspondence and attendance notes between the council and local residents between January 2005 and October 2007.'

- **Give deadline.** Inform the authority that you expect to hear from it promptly and, in any event, within 20 days. The authority must supply the information in 20 working days if it can (under the laws, there are provisions which authorities can rely on to extend that period).

CASE STUDY: OLD SODBURY COMPOST FARM ACTION GROUP

Julia Coulthard, chair of Old Sodbury Compost Farm Action Group, has found the freedom of information provisions a powerful tool in her group's campaign against the development of a waste composting site.

'We've found that many council and environment agency officers have been slow to understand how the legislation operates and slow to fulfil their obligations,' says Coulthard. 'We have had to explain to them: "You have to do this a certain way". The difficulty we found ourselves in at times was that we simply did not know what information the council or the agency held. It was necessary to explain our particular problem over the telephone and then discuss it with the officer. Often council and agency officers became interested in trying to solve the case of the missing information with you.'

Coulthard points out that often 'officers will do anything to get people and problems off their back. But when making personal contact by telephone always take the time to explain the nature of your issue with them,' she says. 'Do not be afraid to ask questions, but realise that you are probably dealing with a small team that is under-resourced. This can actually be a bonus in terms of the broader campaign because you may well find that someone along the line could be cutting corners. If so, the proper procedures may not have been followed and the decision or action that you are challenging is, in fact, unlawful.'

It pays to be polite. 'You can usually build up a good relationship with information officers,' concludes Coulthard. 'It is their job to find out and investigate matters. If they can successfully help you, then there must be some job satisfaction in that.'

Personal inspection

You are entitled to attend a public authority's offices to personally inspect those documents that you are seeking. One real benefit of inspecting files is that you have a better chance of satisfying yourself not only about what's in the file but also what isn't; for example, an unlawful failure to take a decision that an authority is required to take could be evidenced by the fact that a particular file simply doesn't refer to that decision whatsoever. A lack of documentation will also suggest that there has been poor management of the matter in dispute.

If you are going to attend an office to personally inspect files, make an appointment, and make sure you take plenty of post-it notes, notepaper and cash to pay for photocopying as necessary. Also, leave yourself time to review the files properly.

Watch out for any documents that may have been altered. It is an offence to alter, deface or conceal any record held by a public body, with the intention of preventing the disclosure of information by that authority. There is a maximum £5,000 fine.

Cost

The public body providing information is entitled to charge a reasonable amount for providing that information, but government guidance says that the public sector should bear most of the cost. For this reason, the FOIA allows authorities to turn down requests for information on the grounds that it is too expensive for them to comply with the request. A public authority cannot charge more than £600 if it is a central government body or £450 for others (2008 figures). It should also use the same hourly rate, currently £25 per hour, when estimating staff-time costs, regardless of the actual costs. If the estimated cost of providing the information exceeds the cost limit, then the public body can refuse the request. Bear in mind that these figures are the 'limit' and you will only be charged the actual costs of copying, printing and postage.

If the public authority is seeking to charge what you consider to be an excessive amount, stand your ground and explain that such a charge is contrary to the principle of open government and the right to information. In most cases, photocopying and printing would be expected to cost no more than 10p per copy. Some public bodies, notably local authorities, still try to charge excessive amounts for photocopying. If you feel it's too much, refer them to paragraph 3.4.5 of the Department of Constitutional Affairs (now Ministry of Justice) online guidance at www.dca.gov.uk.

Further detail is available at www.justice.gov.uk (Guidance on the Application of the Freedom of Information and Data Protection (Appropriate Limit and Fees) Regulations 2004).

WHAT COSTS ARE REASONABLE?

Say, for example, you are inspecting documents relating to the planning application at your council's planning department. After inspection you ask for photocopies, only to be told it will cost £6 for each building control or planning decision notice plus 50p per page. You believe this is unreasonable. What's fair?

These are the facts of a case in 2006 called *Markinson v Commissioner*. Markinson believed such costs were unreasonable and complained to the Information Commissioner. The Commissioner agreed with the council. The case then went to the Information Tribunal, the court that hears appeals from the Information Commissioner. The Tribunal concluded that the Commissioner had not applied the correct test to determine its charges and directed the council to reassess. It offered as a guide the rate of 10p per page. It said that the council 'should be free to exceed that guide price figure only if it can demonstrate that there is a good reason for it to do so'.

How to challenge a refusal

If a public body fails to provide the information you have requested, you can challenge it. The first step is to ask the authority to review its decision to refuse. A request must be made within 40 working days after you were told of the refusal (the review process is free of charge). A public body must advise of its review decision within 40 days of the date of the request for review.

Appeal to the Information Commissioner

If you still aren't satisfied – perhaps the public body is continuing to unreasonably withhold information or it is simply not responding – then you can go to the Information Commissioner. You must appeal, in writing, within two months of the public authority's decision (or failure to decide). There is no fee for appealing. The Commissioner is independent of the public body and has powers of entry and inspection. This can be an uphill struggle. The freedom of information campaigner Heather Brooke reckons that the Commissioner's investigations 'tend to be remarkably one-sided with the Information Commissioner's Office consulting extensively with the public body but barely at all with the individual complainant'. Brooke notes that the Commissioner's entire budget is 'set directly by the government and not Parliament and so it is also difficult for him to claim to be truly independent'.

If you are not satisfied with the Information Commissioner's decision, then there is a further right of appeal to the Information Tribunal. Any appeal must be made within 28 days of receiving the Commissioner's decision. Again, it is free of charge. You must complete a formal Notice of Appeal, which can be downloaded from the Information Tribunal website.

For more information on the powers of the Information Commissioner see www.ico.gov.uk and www.information tribunal.gov.uk.

To find out more about making requests, visit the Campaign for Freedom of Information website (www.cfoi.org.uk), as well as Heather Brooke's website, www.yrtk.org. See Appendix 5 for Model FOIA request letters.

CHAPTER 8

Law

> 'People shouldn't regard the law as prohibitively expensive. There are specialist lawyers who are willing to work with clients on campaigning issues. You might find lawyers happy to take on your case in ways other than the old-fashioned hourly rate. There is legal aid, "no win, no fee" and other ways that groups can avail themselves of legal help. It doesn't have to cost a fortune.'
>
> David Whiting, chief executive of the Environmental Law Foundation

If your campaign is going to come into contact with the law, then it's most likely going to be in one of two ways. The first is that you might well need to take legal action to further the aims of your campaign; for example, you might want to challenge the questionable decision of your local authority to build a by-pass close to your village. Of the respondents to the questionnaire, a significant minority (about one-third) needed professional legal advice for that reason. The second reason is ensuring that your campaigning activities stay on the right side of the law.

Legal proceedings should always be regarded as a last resort. Going to the courts prematurely is likely to be perceived as unnecessarily aggressive, not to mention a costly and highly risky enterprise.

However, the law might be a necessary last resort. The legal profession is far more approachable than it used to be and there are more funding options (despite the shrinking of legal aid) than there have been in the past.

This chapter gives a brief overview of the legal system, including who does what and how it works. In particular, it considers challenging public decisions by judicial review as well as looking at areas of potential legal liability. It also looks at legal costs.

CHAPTER OVERVIEW:
• Finding a lawyer
• The law – an overview
• Challenging public authorities
• Other legal action
• Legal liability
• Direct action
• Other approaches

Finding a lawyer

Advice from a legal professional can be pricey, but, as said at the outset of this chapter, legal advice need not be prohibitively expensive these days.

Where to start?

Before approaching a lawyer, you should be aware how diverse a profession the law is and make sure that you approach a lawyer who has the right expertise. The main considerations – all of which will have considerable bearing on the fee your lawyer will charge – are as follows:

- **Type of lawyer/type of firm.** Solicitors (as opposed to barristers) tend to be the public's first point of contact with the profession. They manage a case on a day-to-day basis; whereas barristers are instructed to act as your advocate (in other words, they represent you in court) or give an expert opinion on particular aspects of the law. The separation between the two sides of the profession is not quite so clear as it once was and, for example, there are also solicitor-advocates who have 'rights of audience' (in other words, they can represent you in court).

Lawyers at 'City firms' (i.e. those based in the City of London) tend to specialise in business law for corporate clients and charge the highest rates. Then 'regional' or 'national' firms tend to have both corporate and private clients (i.e. individuals like you and members of your group). They charge more than your local 'high street' firms, which tend to advise individuals, often on issues such as conveyancing, wills and probate. It could well be appropriate for you to go to a large regional firm or a specialist practice (or even a City firm) for expert advice on, for example, environmental law. Telephone directories list local law firms and all firms are listed on the Law Society's website (www.lawsociety.org.uk). To find a specialist lawyer, there are directories (such as www.chambersandpartners.com or www.legal500.com).

- **The lawyer's experience.** Unsurprisingly, the more senior the lawyer the greater the fee they command within a firm. 'Partners' command the greatest fee; other, more junior solicitors are known as 'associates' or 'assistants'; and there are other legally qualified staff such as legal executives, and then paralegals, who undertake legal work without any formal qualification but who can often have considerable experience.

- **The type of work.** The more specialist the area of law, the greater the likely fee.

Legal costs

When you consider the possible expense of instructing a lawyer, you need to consider the following: lawyer's fees (e.g. time spent on your case, telephone calls, letters, etc), expenses (known as disbursements, which will include court fees, barristers' fees and reports) and then there is VAT.

The general rule in our courts is that the loser pays the winner's costs. This means that if you win your case, you are entitled to have your costs paid. But if you lose, you could be liable to pay your opponent's costs. In a judicial review (which is popular with campaign groups for reasons explained later in this chapter), an interested party, such as a developer, may also seek to claim some of their costs from your group. It is the 'loser pays' rule that often dissuades potential claimants, especially campaign groups without money, from pursuing legal action. Sadly, your opponent may be all too aware of this inequality of arms.

The court can use its discretion not to make an order for costs against a losing party in public law cases (in other words, those cases concerning the exercise of power by public authorities) or make what is called a 'protective costs order' (PCO), which is an order early on in the legal proceedings which places a cap limiting the costs your opponent could claim should you lose your case. The courts have been fairly reluctant to grant such orders.

Funding a case

The most common method of charging is 'the hourly rate' – and most solicitors charge in this way. This reflects the time spent by your solicitor dealing with the matter. Hourly rates vary from the high street where a 2007 figure could be £125 to £150 an hour, through to a senior partner in the City where it could be as much as £500 an hour. Increasingly, lawyers are using fixed fees, which have the obvious appeal because they limit your liability for their costs. Although, such an approach is often considered commercially unattractive by lawyers if a case goes to court because of the unpredictability, not least the length of a case. Even so you are still entitled to a best estimate of likely costs under the solicitors' code of conduct.

There are ways, other than the hourly rate, of funding which might be relevant.

Legal aid

You might be entitled to public funding (or legal aid). To qualify for legal aid, you need to ask yourself two questions:

1. **Is your case covered by the legal aid scheme?** Not all cases are. For example, claims for defamation are not (The McLibel Two had to fight a two-and-a-half-year trial unassisted by public funds, except for two hours' free advice at the very start; see chapter 1). Five years ago the government removed all routine accident claims from the scheme.

2. **Are you financially eligible?** If your case is covered by legal aid, you have to be deemed eligible. The criteria are tight. The legal aid scheme is very complicated and there are many caveats and rules, but roughly speaking, to receive financial support in 2007 your income couldn't be more than £649 a month and your capital had to be under £8,000. To find out more about eligibility and how to find a legal aid lawyer visit www.clsdirect.org.uk.

Legal aid is now known formally as 'public funding' although both lawyers and the Legal Services Commission, which administers the scheme, still refer to it as 'legal aid'.

No win, no fee

You may have read the phrase 'no win, no fee' in the press. While the name suggests a very straightforward funding arrangement, it is more complex. Lawyers call such deals 'conditional fee agreements' (CFAs) and they are mainly, but not exclusively, used to fund accident claims; they can be used for a wide range of other legal claims, providing the lawyers are prepared to offer them. This type of agreement allows solicitors to waive fees if they lose (hence 'no win, no fee') and to charge extra if they win. So if you lose, you pay nothing to your own lawyer but technically you are liable to pay the other side's legal fees (under the 'loser pays rule'). However, as part of a CFA, you take out an insurance policy known as 'after-the-event' insurance and, if necessary, you can get a loan to pay the premium. All reasonable costs of the other side, and the solicitor's success fee, should be covered by this premium. 'No win, no fee' doesn't mean 'win, no cost' – in other words, costs could be deducted from any payout. You should be clear that, whatever happens, any compensation is paid back intact if that is appropriate. (Although, more often than not, a campaign-related claim is unlikely to involve a compensation payout.)

Other sources

If you belong to a trade union, or a member of your family does, you may be entitled to have free legal help from your union. For example, Unison offers a free 30-minute telephone interview with a solicitor about any issue. It is also worth looking at your motor or household insurance policies to see if they include legal expenses insurance. Almost all policies exclude cover for judicial review.

There are a number of sources of free legal advice. The Citizens Advice Bureaux has a website (www.adviceguide.org.uk) with advice on many legal and consumer rights issues. If you want to see someone in person, it has 2,000 bureaux, plus there are more than 50 Law Centres, as well as any number of other advice agencies. Check out your *Yellow Pages*. There are other online legal resources such as the Environmental Law Foundation (www.elflaw.org) and Friends of the Earth (www.foe.co.uk).

Lawyers take on some work free of charge. The public can't contact the main group, Solicitors' Pro Bono Group, directly, but for more information see www.lawworks.org.uk.

The law – an overview

Our law comprises legislation enacted by Parliament and case law arising from court decisions. However, you should be aware that UK law is constantly evolving. It may be amended, repealed or interpreted by the courts. An overview of the legal system is provided below.

It is important to be aware that the legal systems in England and Wales are separate from Scotland and Northern Ireland. The legal position in England and Wales is not necessarily the same north of the border. You should also be aware that as members of the European Union (EU), there is a body of European law that might have a relevance to your campaign. EU law can be found at www.europa.eu.int. Our legal system has to be compliant with EU legislation when it introduces new laws. Also, all public bodies including government departments and local authorities must act consistently with EU law, regardless of whether or not there is UK law on the same point. The EU has an increasingly important role to play in our national law, particularly in relation to matters such as the environment, employment, and consumer protection.

Legislation

UK legislation includes statutes (in other words, 'Acts of Parliament') and regulations made under them (known as 'Statutory Instruments'). Virtually all UK legislation currently in force is now available online at www.statutelaw.gov.uk.

Case law

We live in a 'common law' legal system. In other words, our law is based upon the principle of applying precedents set by previous judicial decisions. This body of law built up in the courts is known as 'case law'. Our courts interpret the law with reference to the decisions of earlier similar cases. Judges are bound to follow the earlier reasoning unless there are good reasons to depart from it. When the courts are asked to decide points of dispute between two or more sides (or 'parties'), they will decide the case upon the facts presented to them. They will often interpret the legislation and provide judgments clarifying points of law. If there is an absence of clarity in the legislation, the courts look to previous case law. The level of judicial authority afforded to an earlier decision depends on the court making the decision. The higher up the legal hierarchy the decision is made, the greater authority the case is given – see below.

An upper court can choose to follow a lower court decision but it is not bound to follow it. All lower court decisions, however, should be consistent with the upper courts. If not, it is likely that its decisions could be appealed.

Court system

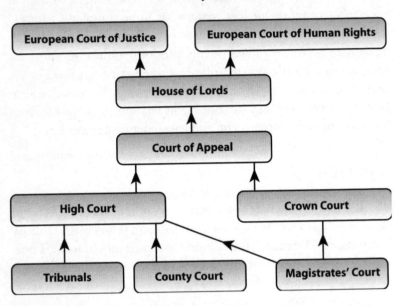

A large number of court decisions are now available online. Most High Court and Court of Appeal cases can be found at www.bailii.org. All House of Lords decisions can be found at www.parliament.gov.uk. All European Court of Justices cases are available at www.curia.europa.eu. All European Court of Human Rights cases are at www.echr.coe.int.

If your campaign looks like it is heading for the courts, then you need legal advice.

Challenging public authorities

Public law refers to the rules and principles governing the exercise of power by public authorities. Campaigners may, for example, want to challenge a decision made by their local authority to close a school or to grant permission for the development of an incinerator. Those decisions are covered by public law. In such cases, the public authority must act within its powers or according to its legal duties and correct legal principles. If such a body reaches a decision which is in breach of those principles, then you might be able to challenge that decision.

The main ways of challenging such a decision by a public body are as follows:

- make an official complaint using its complaint procedures;

- complain to the relevant ombudsman (you would usually have to go through the above complaints procedure first);

- ask the public body to go to mediation (or use some other form of 'alternative dispute resolution');

- use a tribunal or statutory appeal (if available);

- ask a court to examine the decision by judicial review if there is no suitable alternative remedy;

- petition the European Parliament (if the matter covers an area of European law) – see chapter 5.

For more information see the Public Law Project (a charity which aims to improve access to public law remedies) or view its website at www.publiclawproject.org.uk.

The best approach is to try to come to some sort of resolution with the public authority by starting with an informal complaint first; however, you should also bear in mind that if you are going to bring a judicial review then you need to act swiftly.

Judicial review

The judicial review (JR) can be an important weapon for the campaigner – it's sometimes known as 'the citizen's weapon'. For example, a decision by the Environment Agency to grant a pollution permit for a controversial new incinerator in Peacehaven, East Sussex, was overturned (or 'quashed') in December 2007 by the High Court – because the Agency failed to take into account the impact of emissions on global warming and climate change. Without such permit, the incinerator cannot operate.

You will need specialist advice before bringing a claim for JR. It is the examination by the court of an administrative decision to determine whether the decision has been made properly. It is not about the merits of any decision (whether the decision by the public authority is good or bad – that is almost entirely at the discretion of that authority). As such it is a vital check on the conduct of public bodies and how they go about their duties. The focus of the High Court (where JRs are heard) therefore is on the powers of the public authority that made the decision or the decision-making process itself, rather than the correctness of the decision. As almost all campaigning relates to public actions and decisions, the JR will be a likely form of legal action a campaign group might consider.

Who can use JR?

You, as a potential claimant, must have 'sufficient interest' in the decision or action being challenged. The courts have applied a wide interpretation of 'sufficient interest', so in the case of, for example, controversial proposals for a new incinerator, this might include not only neighbours but parish councils and non-governmental organisations (NGOs). In one case called *R v Inspectorate of Pollution ex p Greenpeace Ltd*, Greenpeace challenged the permission granted to British Nuclear Fuels for the discharge of radioactive waste by the Pollution Inspectorate (now the Environment Agency). When considering whether a campaigning group like Greenpeace had 'sufficient interest' to bring the review, as distinct from concerned locals, the judge concluded that if he were to deny its right to bring the challenge 'those it represents might not have an effective way to bring the issues before the court'. The judge said that a restrictive definition would have meant only an application by an employee or a neighbour could have proceeded. He went on to say, 'in this case, it is unlikely that either would be able to command the expertise which is at the disposal of Greenpeace. Consequently, a less well-informed challenge might be mounted.' The conclusion by the judge meant that Greenpeace was allowed to bring the action.

The defendant will be the government department, council or other public body taking the decision. Any other organisation or individual likely to be directly affected by a court order will be included in the claim as 'an interested party'. For example, in challenging the grant of planning permission by your local council, the defendant will be the council and the interested party will be the developer.

Assessing whether you have a good case

As said earlier, JR is only concerned with the correctness of the decision-making process, not the rights and wrongs of any decision. The legal grounds for a review have been defined by the courts as unlawfulness, unfairness and unreasonableness:

- 'Unlawfulness' includes, among other things, illegality, error of law, abuse of power as well as breaches of the Human Rights Act 1998.

- 'Unfairness' includes procedural impropriety (e.g. malice or dishonesty), bias and the right to a fair hearing.

- 'Unreasonableness' includes conduct so unreasonable or irrational that no sensible person taking the decision in question could lawfully have arrived at the decision reached.

You should bear in mind that courts start from the principle that the decision (that can be an act or a failure to act) should not be overturned and therefore you must prove on 'a balance of probabilities' (in other words, more likely than not) why the decision is incorrect.

It is very important to stress when considering JR that the legal proceedings must be started as soon as possible – and in any event within three months of the decision being challenged.

The hearing

JR proceedings are relatively straightforward, but specialist advice is needed as mentioned earlier, and relies mainly on written documents and legal submissions. It is pretty rare for anyone to actually give spoken evidence in the courtroom. Hearings may take anything from half a day up to one week, although one or two days are common in most cases. Sometimes, judgment is given immediately, although generally it is given a few days later.

The decision

The court can make the following kind of orders:

- a mandatory order, requiring a public body to carry out a particular duty;
- a prohibiting order, preventing a public body from acting or continuing to act unlawfully (it is similar to an injunction);
- a quashing order, which has the effect of overturning the decision being challenged (the most common outcome) and either sending the matter to the decision-maker or directing it to reconsider and reach a decision in line with the judgment;
- an injunction, restraining a person from acting in any office in which they are not entitled to act;
- a declaration setting out the legal position; and
- an order to pay damages (although that is rare and usually would be in a situation where there has been a breach of someone's human rights).

Other legal action

While public law is without doubt the most common form of legal action for campaigners, it is by no means the only legal avenue. It may be appropriate to bring legal proceedings in employment law if, for example, an employee has been sacked for whistleblowing (in other words, highlighting malpractice in the workplace for the good of employees and the public). The Public Interest Disclosure Act

1998 protects whistleblowers from dismissal and victimisation. For more information contact the charity Public Concern at Work at www.pcaw.co.uk.

Nuisance

If you are campaigning against a factory or incinerator in your local area and, for example, you are having problems with pollution, you may want to consider bringing legal action directly against the person or company responsible for that problem. There are three kinds of nuisance:

1. **Statutory nuisance.** The starting point with any environmental health problem is that the local council should sort the matter out. They are in some instances under a legal duty to act. Any problem arising has to fit into one of around 12 nuisances that are set out in the Environmental Protection Act 1990 (hence 'statutory' nuisance). Common complaints such as noise and smells can be challenged by the council under this legislation. If your council is unwilling to take action in statutory nuisance, any person that is 'aggrieved' by the problem may bring legal proceedings directly.

2. **Private nuisance.** If you are affected by a problem such as smoke or smells and have some interest in the property (e.g. if you rent or own property in the area), you can start legal proceedings in private nuisance. The court can grant an injunction to stop the problem or award compensation. Therefore, it may be worth considering, particularly if your local council is not prepared to act.

3. **Public nuisance.** This is brought by the local authority and is, in practice, quite rare. The problem needs to affect a reasonable section of the community.

Legal liability

There is the potential for campaigners to fall foul of both the criminal and civil law. This section sets out those areas that might (but hopefully won't) apply to you and your fellow campaigners. You might want to check out Appendix 6, which comprises the civil rights group Liberty's *Your Right to Peaceful Protest – A guide*.

Criminal liability

There will be few campaigns that set out to intentionally break the law. However, some demos, pickets and direct action skirt close to the edge of the law and could end up with campaign members committing public order offences, such as affray, offensive conduct or obstruction of a highway. The main public order offences under the Public Order Act 1986 (POA) are set out below. You could end up in prison for committing a number of these offences.

- **Affray.** A person is guilty of affray if they use violence or even threaten someone in such a way that would cause someone else at the scene to fear for their own safety. For instance, if a group of campaigners at a particularly rowdy demo are shouting, threatening each other, fighting, wielding placards, and other people close by, but not actually part of the fighting group, are distressed by this, then those fighting could find themselves guilty of the offence. The maximum penalty is three years' imprisonment and/or a fine.

- **Violent disorder.** Violent disorder is where at least three or more people use or threaten violence to such an extent that someone witnessing the scene fears for their own safety. This could be, for example, if there was fighting between groups of people. If convicted, the maximum penalty is five years' imprisonment and/or a fine.

- **Riot.** This is where 12 or more people use or threaten violence for a common purpose and to the extent that someone witnessing the scene or event would fear for their own safety. There were the infamous poll tax riots in Trafalgar Square in central London in 1990 and more recently riots in 2003 when white and Asian men clashed following a British National Party demonstration in Bradford. During these incidents, police officers were attacked and stolen cars set alight. The activities were filmed and more than 100 defendants were convicted, some with sentences of between four and six years. The maximum penalty for riot is ten years' imprisonment and/or a fine. Importantly, it is irrelevant whether or not all the people involved in the riotous activity are being violent. The common aim or purpose may be inferred from carrying banners, shouting and making verbal threats.

- **Fear or provocation of violence.** The offence occurs when someone uses threatening, abusive or insulting words or behaviour towards someone else, for instance, by distributing leaflets or displaying signs. In fact, it covers any writing or sign. There has to be an intention so that a victim might believe that violence will be used against them. The courts have held that letters containing the threat of a bombing campaign could constitute an offence and that the immediate fear of violence does not have to be instantaneous. The maximum penalty for the offence of fear or provocation of violence is six months' imprisonment and/or a £5,000 fine.

- **Intentional harassment, alarm or distress.** A person will commit an offence if they intentionally cause someone else harassment, alarm or distress by using threatening, abusive or insulting words or behaviour. The maximum penalty is six months' imprisonment and/or a £5,000 fine. The crucial aspect of this offence is that there must be intention to cause harassment but such intent could be inferred, for instance, by abuse shouted when in a large crowd, even though that crowd may not actually be acting in a violent manner.

- **Obstruction of the highway.** If you are organising a demo or a march, it is an offence under the Highways Act 1980 to intentionally obstruct a highway and so restrict free passage of either vehicles or people unless justified. The maximum penalty is a £1,000 fine.

- **Public processions.** If you are organising a demo or a march, you must give at least six days' written notice of the date, time and route of an intended procession. Failure to provide advance notice is an offence, unless it was not reasonably practicable to provide such notice. The maximum penalty is a £1,000 fine. Under Sections 12 and 13 of the POA, the police can either prohibit or place conditions on any public procession.

There are exceptions to the requirement to give notice, in particular if the processions are held regularly. The question of when a procession is regularly held was looked at by the Court of Appeal in 2007 in a case called *Commissioner of Police for the Metropolis v Desmond Woolf Kay*, which decided that the monthly cycle ride in London organised by the campaigners' group Critical Mass, which was held on the last Friday of each month starting at the same place but taking different routes, was not regularly held.

- **Aggravated trespass and trespassory assembly.** A person commits an offence of aggravated trespass if they enter someone else's land without permission and then intimidate or obstruct others who are themselves carrying on a lawful activity. In 2001, protestors were arrested and charged with aggravated trespass when they entered a field in which genetically modified (GM) crops were being trialled and began uprooting the crops. In doing so, they were regarded as obstructing the GM trial. The maximum penalty is three months' imprisonment and/or a £2,500 fine. (Criminal Justice and Public Order Act 1994, Section 68.)

  The police can restrict or ban any assembly if they believe it's being held on land that the public has no right of access to and if they are concerned that there may be damage to the land, buildings or a disturbance to others. It is an offence under Section 14B of the POA to take part in an assembly which has been expressly prohibited. If convicted, the maximum penalty is 51 weeks and/or a £2,500 fine.

  These aggravated trespass offences are distinct from the civil form of trespass, which is discussed below and may be pursued by individuals to prevent a person entering or remaining on land.

- **Demonstrations.** Many of the offences above cover aspects of demonstrations. However, recent laws have sought to specifically restrict demonstrations in certain designated areas – for example, around Houses of Parliament. Any demo has to be authorised by the police. For example, at the time of going to press, the powers-that-be have yet to shift anti-war protester Brian Haw from his makeshift home of almost six years in Parliament Square, Westminster, despite provisions under the Serious Organised Crime and Police Act 2005 being introduced with the sole purpose of bringing to an end his vigil which began in July 2001.

- **Breaking up a public meeting.** It is an offence for anyone to act in a disorderly manner at a public meeting with a view to disrupting that meeting, for example, the AGM of a company or a council's committee meeting. The maximum penalty if found guilty is six months' imprisonment or a £5,000 fine. It is also an offence under the Act to incite others to do the same. (Public Meeting Act 1908, Section 1.)

Defences to criminal offences

There are a number of defences that could be relied upon if someone is charged with one of the offences mentioned above. For instance, obstruction of the highway is not an offence if you have lawful authority or excuse to do so. If it was not reasonably practicable to provide advance notice of a procession, the offence is not committed. You should make sure you check the detailed provisions in the statute that creates the offence in case there is a justification for your action.

The above list includes those offences which are most likely to arise from campaigning activity. There may be others that the police or prosecutor could use. You could, for instance, be charged with assault, if you put a person in fear of being physically attacked in some form or another.

It is also important to note that the government is always finding new ways to further regulate or outlaw public demonstration. If there is any doubt about a proposed campaign action or event being lawful, you should seek legal advice about it before you go ahead.

Civil liability

Outside of the criminal law, campaigners might need to be aware of the following:

- **Trespass.** Trespass occurs when one person enters someone else's land without their permission or a justifiable excuse. Trespass also occurs if anything is placed on someone's land or damage is done to it.

  You can trespass whether or not you realise that you are trespassing. However, there are defences (consent, necessity and lawful authority) that may be available in limited circumstances. Monsanto sued anti-GM activists for trespass. The activists claimed that they were acting out of necessity to prevent the widespread use of GM crops. The court decided that the defence of necessity would only apply if they had acted in the face of immediate and serious danger to life and where their actions were reasonable – clearly that was not the case. The activists were found liable and were prohibited from re-entering the land. A successful trespass claim will result in the court granting an injunction or damages. A landowner can use reasonable force to resist trespass.

- **Defamation.** Campaigners are, by nature, forthright in expressing their opinions – in their literature and speaking to the public and press. It is important that any statement made is not defamatory to any person or company. Defamation is a wrong or injury to a living person's reputation or character so that a right-thinking citizen would think less of them as a result of the wrong. If it is written down or in 'some other permanent form' (which according to the law could include material recorded for TV, radio or Internet broadcast), then it is called libel. That does not mean that you cannot criticise a company or organisation, but ensure that what you say is accurate, truthful and, preferably, objective.

  The distinction between the two is important because a person can sue for libel without proof of any damage or harm to reputation. However, for slander there must be some evidence that a person's reputation has been harmed.

If someone is claiming that you have made a defamatory statement, you may be able to rely upon a number of defences, such as:

- a lack of intention (if you can prove that you did not intend to make the defamatory statement you might have the opportunity to apologise publicly and conclude the matter out of court); or

- the other party consented to the statement; or

- it could also be argued that the statement made was justified or true; or

- that the statement was a fair comment (the matter commented on must be of public interest, it must an expression of opinion, not a statement of fact and the comment must be fair); or that

- the statement was made in parliamentary proceedings or in court.

- **Negligence and breach of contract.** You should also be aware that as a group you could be liable for actions that are only indirectly linked to your campaign; for example, not paying an invoice for goods will be a breach of contract and organising a meeting or rally where someone is injured could result in a claim in negligence.

Direct action

Government, councils and organisations fearful of the impacts of direct action can sometimes apply to the court to obtain an injunction, which as mentioned before is a court order compelling someone to stop doing something. However, the extent and scope of any injunction must be reasonable. An example in which the court limited such an order was in the Climate Camp demos in the summer of 2007 when the British Airports Authority (BAA) sought to ban a vast range of groups and people from protesting against climate change at or around Heathrow airport.

CASE STUDY: CLIMATE CHANGE

In August 2007, the British Airports Authority (BAA) applied for an injunction banning organisers of the Camp for Climate Action (or Climate Camp), an umbrella group of environmental and conservation groups, from carrying out a week-long protest near Heathrow. BAA obtained an injunction against three named individuals and a group called 'Plane Stupid', but failed to extend the effect of the injunction to cover a much wider area, including parts of the London Underground system and the land intended to be used to set the camp up.

Although the injunction was a draconian measure the campaigners used it to their advantage. They called it the 'mother of all injunctions' and told the press that it would limit the movements of some five million people, including the judge hearing the application. 'BAA so overplayed their hand, they looked daft,' says campaigner John Stewart, chair of Airport Watch. 'Rather than James Bond, they were Mr Bean. Their response acted as a spur and, ironically, there were many more people at the Climate Camp as a result of what they tried to do.'

If direct action is proposed, then you want to ensure that all campaign members are aware of how to stay within the law. Perhaps it is part of your campaign plan for a group member to be arrested and to use the publicity that this could raise, but you must be clear as to the implications of arrest for that individual and the campaign group; for example, being fined, put in prison and being left with a criminal record.

Other approaches

As said at the outset of this chapter, legal action should always be regarded as a last resort. There may be occasions where legal proceedings can be avoided in favour of an out-of-court approach – known as Alternative Dispute Resolution (ADR). For campaigning, there are two main potential alternatives to legal proceedings – mediation and negotiation. Each involves an element of compromise. You must, however, be certain that embarking on ADR does not later prevent you from starting legal proceedings; for example, because you have missed a time limit for issuing proceedings. If there is a risk, you should issue proceedings and then agree to halt (or 'stay') the matter to allow ADR to proceed.

- **Mediation.** It allows you and your opponent to reach an agreement that may be acceptable to you both with the help of a third party mediator. It can help to clarify points of dispute and focus on your real concerns, as well as help to explore appropriate settlements. Mediation is confidential and without prejudice to your rights, unless you are committed to a formal settlement agreement which is signed by the parties and converted into a court order. It can be inexpensive and highly effective. It can take place either before a legal action has begun or in the time leading up to a hearing. The mediator does not propose solutions. They leave this up to you and your opponent in order that you can jointly 'own' any settlement achieved.

  For more information, see the National Mediation Helpline (www.nationalmediation), Centre for Dispute Resolution (www.cedr.co.uk) and UK mediation (www.ukmediation.net).

- **Negotiation.** This is a technique in which you and your opponent deal with each other directly, with or without legal representatives. For more formal negotiation, you should have an idea of the very least that you hope to achieve – the bottom line. You should also set your 'best alternative to a negotiated agreement' (BATNA), which will help to focus your mind if negotiation breaks down. In some situations your BATNA may be a total breakdown of the relationship or having to issue court proceedings. When considering a party's BATNA, the absolute bottom line may shift.

An example of ADR campaigning is where local residents object to a particular activity but where no formal decision (such as the grant of planning permission for a multi-storey high rise) has been taken in relation to that activity. In this way any organisation such as a developer should be aware that the local community has raised concerns. To find out more about the use of ADR in environmental campaigning, you can visit the website of the Environment Council (www.the-environment-council.org.uk).

CASE STUDY: DENHOLME RESIDENTS' ACTION GROUP

Denholme Residents' Action Group (DRAG) was formed in 1999 to oppose the development of a nearby quarry for landfill. The campaign has been involved in a planning inquiry and three court cases, including a visit. Sharon Makinson, the group's chair, explains the need for legal action.

'We knew that we would have to try and raise some sort of fighting fund. We've been overwhelmed by the public response. We are not an affluent village and a high proportion of residents rely on state benefits or they're in low wage jobs. At our first meeting we collected just over £250. The largest expense has, without doubt, been our legal costs despite the fact that one of the residents was granted legal aid to pursue the case. This is because even if one resident is granted legal aid, others will be expected to make a contribution to legal costs. We've always paid for these costs and others from our own pockets as we have gone along.

The legal action began in earnest after the council refused planning permission. The developer then appealed and there was a planning inquiry. This was in 2001. We represented ourselves at the planning inquiry because we couldn't afford lawyers. The council had refused the application, and the developer appealed. At the inquiry the council's planning officers refused to attend and left it to us to defend the appeal of the developer on our own. We had the passion, the local support and the will to oppose the development, but we were aware that we would also need someone that understood mining extraction and waste operations. The Mineral Planning Group, a waste and minerals consultant, helped at the planning inquiry and gave expert evidence on our behalf.

We were convinced in 2001 that the development would get turned down, but that was not to be. We felt there were fundamental problems with the environmental assessment and that the Inspector's decision was unlawful. We decided to challenge the Inspector's decision in court. We did this by a kind of judicial review peculiar to planning inspectors' decisions called "statutory review". That was quite an intense time. We had just six weeks to prepare a case. We instructed specialist planning and public law solicitors and barristers.

When the judge dismissed our claim we felt cheated. We believed that the court had made a mistake. We obtained a legal opinion and were told that there were grounds of appeal. The appeal had to be on a point of law – in other words, that the judge had got the law wrong in reaching his decision.

In 2003, the Court of Appeal judges explained that they had serious reservations about the proposal. In the end, however, the judges dismissed our appeal. The developer had permission to start operations, providing it complied with a number of conditions called "conditions precedent" and they had five years in which to submit these.

As time went on, nothing happened at the quarry and ownership of the site also changed hands. Then in 2005 about six months before the planning permission was due to expire, the new owner applied for approval for its plans. We had not been advised that the plans had been submitted for approval and found out more by chance. As soon as we found out we asked the Mineral Planning Group to review them. Their conclusion was that, while superficially, they appeared OK, there were gaps, and as a result any approval by the council would be unlawful. It was certainly clear to us that the plans had been rushed. Then, with less than three weeks before the permission was due to expire, the council approved all the plans and reckoned that the "conditions precedent" were complied with.

We felt that all our hard work and efforts over the previous seven years were about to come undone. The Mineral Planning Group advised us to get legal advice. Once again, we were advised that there had been some unlawfulness in the decision-making process and we decided to start legal proceedings, this time against the council for unlawfully approving the developer's plans. In November 2006, the court held that the council had been unlawful in approving an inadequate landscaping plan. The consequence of this was significant. Not only was the plan inadequate, but the whole planning permission granted in 2001 had now expired and, if the developer wanted to proceed it would have to apply for a completely fresh planning permission.

In June 2007, the developer issued legal proceedings against the council for, in effect, agreeing with the High Court and the legal process continues. There is no certainty that the court will continue to oppose the use of the quarry as a waste site.

There is now a much greater emphasis on recycling and avoiding landfill. It is clear to us that developing a waste site so close to people's homes is wrong and we know that if we are going to resolve the problem in the end we will continue having to fight for what we believe is right, even if it means turning to the courts.'

CHAPTER 9

Making the difference

Local campaigners are often depicted as embattled 'Davids' locked into interminable conflicts with the faceless and uncaring 'Goliaths' of business and government, often without a sling between them.

How effective can campaigning be? Take heart; most of the groups that we interviewed in the research for this book clearly saw themselves as on the winning side. We did not consciously target success stories, but contacted a mixture of local groups that we knew or were aware of, reflecting a wide cross-section of interests.

The reality is that people don't like to devote their time to lost causes. For reasons discussed throughout the book, we are living in a time where local communities are increasingly encouraged to voice their concerns and that creates an expectation of change. For the most part, the campaigners we spoke to were in high spirits; they considered the fight to be worth the effort, and the possibility of positive change not on the distant horizon but within reach. That isn't to say we didn't encounter considerable anger and frustration about, for example, the perceived failings of our overly bureaucratic planning system, overly cautious elected representatives, or the seeming indifference of big business. Unsurprisingly, there was plenty of that.

However, it seems appropriate to end this book by looking at what campaigners have achieved through their energy and commitment. The rest of this chapter looks at the concrete changes brought about by the various campaigns discussed throughout the book.

Success stories

Where to start? One particularly vivid and effective example of 'people power' is the Merton Parents for Better Food in School, which has helped transform and improve the quality of the school dinners in the South London borough of Merton (see chapter 1). The campaign, as so many effective local actions tend to do, successfully tapped into concerns expressed more widely. On this occasion, it was the growing anxiety about the poor quality food that our children eat when at school which was brought forcefully to the national consciousness by the TV chef Jamie Oliver. Jackie Schneider, a parent and teacher, felt her children's school meals were not good enough. So she started a campaign with a petition. She collected 3,000 signatures and asked fellow parents who else wanted to be involved. She was contacted by 150 parents who wanted to be active members and she was off.

What was achieved? Schneider replies that the biggest achievement was 'making the issue transparent because the local authority was getting away with murder'. More specifically, she says the campaign helped to secure money for 39 kitchens to be built in the borough. The parents have also managed to get rid of the old underperforming school dinner contractor and draw up new food specifications for all 40 primary schools in the area.

'This story illustrates to me the way campaigning can change the individual,' said the government minister Ed Miliband about Schneider, who won the Sheila McKechnie Award for consumer action for the campaign. 'The individual can mobilise a movement. And the movement can change policy. It is the best argument against the futility of politics…The course of history can change even when the odds seem overwhelming.'

The odds of being able to change minds in a debate where the sides are so entrenched such as the rights and wrongs of animal testing would have a few years ago seemed overwhelming. One of the most unexpected success stories in campaign terms has been the one on behalf of those speaking up for animal testing. As discussed in chapter 6, it took a 16-year-old from Swindon, called Laurie Pycroft, to kick-start a campaign in favour of vivisection which eminent scientists such as Robert Winston and the neurosurgeon Tipu Aziz signed up to as well as Tony Blair. Pycroft launched Pro-Test from his bedroom via a website and blog. A month later, he led a march of 800 demonstrators through Oxford calling for the right to conduct medical research on animals. Tom Holder, one of the students involved in Pro-Test, sees the success of the campaign as about changing attitudes. It is a campaign through which one commentator noted 'a silent majority found a voice'. A teenager in his bedroom had managed to succeed where the might of the pharmaceutical industry and the near infinite resources of its PR machine had failed in winning the moral high-ground from those most tireless of campaigners – animal rights activists.

Ban Foie Gras is another campaign which started off as a one-man band and launched itself out of cyberspace. The controversial bird liver product which involves the force-feeding of geese is banned from being produced in the UK and the campaign is calling for a ban to be extended to shops and restaurants that sell it. Paul Blanchard, a Labour councillor for York, admitted to being taken aback by how well-received the message was. Within a few months of launching the website, York City Council became the first council in the UK to pass a motion condemning the sale of the bird liver gourmet product anywhere in the city and over 100 MPs signed up to an early-day motion (EDM) calling for an outright ban. 'I have discovered my joy for campaigning through this,' says Blanchard. 'I took it on because I believed in it and it was an issue that struck a chord with me.' *People Power* attests to how energised campaigners have become through their campaigns.

Sadly our book doesn't reveal any such dramatic success stories when it comes to the impenetrable planning process. For the main part our campaigners are in it for the long haul. Change takes time, requires tenacity and needs real strategic thinking to deliver change.

To take one example, DRAG (Denholme Residents' Association Group) have been fighting attempts to use a local quarry for landfill since 1999. There have been various clashes with the planning system, two High Court challenges and one visit to the Court of Appeal. But the fight is worth the effort and the stakes are high. The residents don't want to live on top of a rubbish tip, nor do they want their children to. 'A major source of motivation has been the continuing suspect manoeuvres by the operators,' says Sharon Makinson (see chapter 1). 'This has angered us and anger is a good motivator.'

As the book was being written towards the end of 2007, a one-woman campaign put the little south Devon village of Modbury on the map. As discussed in chapter 5, the camerawoman Rebecca Hosking returned from filming wildlife in the Pacific, having seen first hand the devastating effects that plastic bags can have on marine life and decided that the people that she grew up among had a responsibility to do something. In less than one month Hosking, with the help of friends and footage of what she had filmed, persuaded all 43 Modbury shopkeepers to replace the plastic bags with reusable cloth bags. It is reckoned that they have avoided 500,000 plastic bags ending up in the environment.

This campaign kick-started a plastic-bag-free movement around the UK as communities look to binning plastic bags once and for all (including up to 33 London boroughs). 'Politicians might rue another missed bus, and most of the rest of us may wish they offered more determined leadership on the environment,' said one newspaper leader about the Modbury campaign. 'But at least civil society, which sometimes seems to be dying a lingering death, still has the capacity to flare into life when it can see what to do and how to do it.' It's a point well-made, but our evidence suggests that civil society 'flares into life' more often than that commentator suggests.

We hope that you find the information contained in this book useful.

Good luck.

APPENDIX 1

The *People Power* questionnaire

Over the summer of 2007 the following questionnaire was sent out to various local campaign groups. We contacted around 20 groups who responded to the questions we asked and interviewed them about their experiences, what worked in their campaigns and what did not. It is those experiences that have informed the writing of this book.

We are writing a book on local community action and campaigning. We are hoping to include a series of case studies to highlight the reality of local action. We would be grateful if you could help by answering the questions set out below.

We thank you for your time in supporting what we hope will be a valuable resource for anyone hoping to take positive action. When complete please return the form by email, fax or post to the details at the end of this form.

YOUR CAMPAIGN

1. When was your group set up?

   _____

   _____

   _____

2. What is the purpose of your campaign?

   _____

   _____

   _____

MANAGEMENT

3. How many members does your group have?

_____

_____

_____

4. How is the group structured (i.e. do you have an informal
or corporate structure)?

_____

_____

_____

RALLYING THE TROOPS

5. How does the campaign sustain itself, e.g. maintain/increase
membership, keep active or motivated?

_____

_____

_____

FUNDING

6. What overheads do you incur?

_____

_____

_____

7. How much does it cost to keep your campaign going?

_____

_____

_____

8. What are the most effective forms of fundraising?

_____

_____

_____

PUTTING THE CAMPAIGN INTO ACTION

9. What have been the most effective strategies in terms of achieving the group's aims?

_____

_____

_____

10. How do you keep the press interested?

_____

_____

_____

11. Is there campaign literature and promotional material (e.g. flyers, pamphlets, t-shirts, etc)?

_____

_____

_____

12. Have you had demonstrations or public meetings? If so, how successful have they been?

_____

_____

_____

13. Do you have your own website? If so, could you please provide a) the address, and b) details of how it was set up and maintained.

_____

_____

_____

ACCESS TO INFORMATION

14. Has access to information been an issue during the campaign (e.g. finding out more about planning applications or requests under the Freedom of Information Act)?

_____

_____

_____

15. If so, how effective have your attempts been?

_____

_____

_____

LAW

16. Has legal action been part of the campaign strategy?

_____

_____

_____

17. If so, what kind of legal proceedings have you pursued?

_____

_____

_____

18. How have you paid lawyers (do you pay fees, or are you advised on a 'no win, no fee' basis or legal aid?)?

_____

_____

_____

GENERAL

19. Have you been surprised by the public response and progress you have made (or shocked at the lack of either)?

_____

_____

_____

20. What has been the greatest achievement of the campaign?

_____

_____

_____

21. What has been the most difficult barrier to your success?

_____

_____

_____

22. Finally, please provide any further information about your campaign, challenge or action that you think may be of interest or of value to highlight.

_____

_____

_____

Please confirm whether or not you would agree to us using your campaign as a case study.

Signed _____

Date_____

Please return the completed questionnaire:
by email: _____
by post: _____

Thank you for your time.
Jon Robins
Paul Stookes
20 June 2007

APPENDIX 2

This Appendix comprises the model constitution referred to throughout chapter 1. It is reproduced with the permission of Voluntary Action Sheffield (www.vas.org).

MODEL CONSTITUTION

1. **Name**

   The name of the Group shall be

   _____

2. **Aim**

   The aim of the Group shall be to

   _____

3. **Powers**

   In order to achieve its aim the Group may:

   a. Raise money

   b. Open bank accounts

   c. Acquire and run buildings

   d. Take out insurance

   e. Employ staff

   f. Organise courses and events

   g. Work with similar Groups and exchange information and advice with them

---

h. Do anything that is lawful which will help it to fulfil its aim.

4. **Membership**

a. Membership of the Group shall be open to any individual over eighteen without regards to disability, political or religious affiliation, race, sex or sexual orientation who is:

- interested in helping the Group to achieve its aim;

- willing to abide by the rules of the Group; and

- willing to pay any subscription agreed by the Management Committee.

b. The membership of any member may be terminated for good reason by the Management Committee: Provided that the member concerned shall have the right to be heard by the Management Committee, accompanied by a friend, before a final decision is made.

5. **Management**

a. The Group shall be administered by a Management Committee of not less than three and not more than _____ individuals elected at the Group's Annual General Meeting (AGM).

b. The Officers of the Management Committee shall be: the Chairperson, the Treasurer and the Secretary.

c. The Management Committee may co-opt onto the Committee, up to three individuals, in an advisory and non-voting capacity that it feels will help to fulfil the aim of the Group.

d. The Management Committee shall meet at least two times a year.

e. At least three Management Committee members

must be present for a Management Committee meeting to take place.

f. Voting at Management Committee meetings shall be by a show of hands. If there is a tied vote then the Chairperson shall have a second vote.

g. The Management Committee shall have the power to remove any member of the Committee for good and proper reason.

h. The Management Committee may appoint any other member of the Group as a Committee member to fill a vacancy, provided that the maximum prescribed is not exceeded.

6. The Duties of the Officers

a. The duties of the Chairperson shall be to:

- chair meetings of the Committee and the Group;

- represent the Group at functions/meetings that the Group has been invited to; and

- act as the spokesperson of the Group when necessary.

b. The duties of the Secretary shall be to:

- keep a membership list;

- prepare in consultation with the Chairperson the agenda for meetings of the Committee and the Group;

- take and keep minutes of all meetings; and

- collect and circulate any relevant information within the Group.

c. The duties of the Treasurer shall be to:

- supervise the financial affairs of the Group; and

- keep proper accounts that show all monies

received and paid out by the Group.

7. **Finance**

   a. All monies received by or on behalf of the Group shall be applied to further the aim of the Group and for no other purpose.

   b. Any bank accounts opened for the Group shall be in the name of the Group.

   c. Any cheques issued shall be signed by the Treasurer and one other nominated member of the Management Committee.

   d. The Group shall ensure that its accounts are audited or independently examined every year.

   e. The Group may pay reasonable out-of-pocket expenses including travel, childcare and meal costs to members or Management Committee members.

8. **Annual General Meeting**

   a. The Group shall hold an AGM in the month of
   _____.

   b. All members shall be given at least 14 days' notice of the AGM and shall be entitled to attend and vote.

   c. The business of the AGM shall include:

   • receiving a report from the Chairperson on the Group's activities over the year;

   • receiving a report from the Treasurer on the finances of the Group;

   • electing a new Management Committee; and

   • considering any other matter as may be decided.

   d. At least _____ members must be present for the Annual General Meeting and any other General Meeting to take place.

9. **General Meetings**

   a. There shall be two General Meetings (excluding the AGM) each year.

   b. All members shall be entitled to attend and vote.

10. **Special General Meeting**

    A Special General Meeting may be called by the Management Committee or _____ members to discuss an urgent matter. The Secretary shall give all members 14 days' notice of any Special General Meeting together with notice of the business to be discussed.

11. **Alterations to the Constitution**

    Any changes to this Constitution must be agreed by at least two-thirds of those members present and voting at any General Meeting.

12. **Dissolution**

    The Group may be wound up at any time if agreed by two-thirds of those members present and voting at any General Meeting. In the event of winding up, any assets remaining after all debts have been paid shall be given to another Group with a similar aim.

13. **Adoption of the Constitution**

    Until the first AGM takes place the persons whose names, addresses and signatures appear at the bottom of this document shall act as the Management Committee referred to in this constitution.

14. **Delegated Authority**

    The Management Committee shall have the following delegated powers:

    a. to enter into contracts on behalf of the Group to secure the services of an expert consultant providing that the value of such a contract does not exceed [£2,500 plus VAT];

b. to instruct legal representatives on behalf of the group providing such representation does not exceed [£3,000 plus VAT].

15. The Chairperson shall have the following delegated powers:

a. to enter into contracts on behalf of the Group provided that the extent of liability under that contract does not exceed £1,000 plus VAT.

This Constitution was adopted on by

Name _____

Address _____

_____

Signed _____

Name _____

Address _____

_____

Signed _____

Name _____

Address _____

_____

Signed _____

Source: Voluntary Action Sheffield (www.vas.org)

Model press releases

The following model press releases were prepared by Which? and used as part of its Kids' Food Campaign. We are using them to illustrate how a press release should be structured and presented to be effective as discussed in chapter 4.

PRESS RELEASE

Strictly embargoed until Friday 30 March 2007 at 00:01 hrs

Contact Joe Bloggs on 0207 123 1234, email joe.bloggs@which.co.uk

Which? arms parents in battle against junk food marketing

Which? is empowering parents in the fight against junk food with the launch of a **Kids' Food Campaign Toolkit** – a resource to help people combat the promotion of unhealthy foods in their community.

The toolkit, which can be downloaded from **which.co.uk/kidsfood**, highlights some of the tactics companies use to target children with food high in fat, salt and sugar. It also contains advice on how parents can promote the campaign – from getting support from local politicians to gaining coverage in the media.

Miranda Watson, food campaigner, Which? says:

"The marketing of junk food to children goes far beyond television advertising. In some cases, parents may be totally unaware that their children are being targeted.

"If you are a parent and are fed up with being undermined by the irresponsible marketing of unhealthy foods, then you can get involved in our campaign by downloading a toolkit from our website and raising awareness in your local area."

The launch of the toolkit comes ahead of the first phase of new Ofcom regulations that prohibit junk food adverts being shown during television programmes aimed at children. The new regulations don't go far enough, says Which?

Miranda Watson continues:

"Ofcom has let children down. These rules won't cover the programmes most children watch. They will still allow cartoon characters to promote unhealthy foods during programmes such as Coronation Street and Dancing on Ice – when most children are watching - so how will this make a difference? The government needs to take a lead. With an escalating obesity crisis we can't afford for them to wait another couple of years before stepping in."

Notes to editors:

*Fast food brands embedded in popular online games, sugary drinks sponsoring playgrounds and competitions sponsoring confectionery are just a few of the dirty tricks Which? has uncovered.

A Which? survey of 815 parents of 0 – 16 year olds in Great Britain from 9th February to 7th March 2006 found that:

> 8 out of 10 parents think TV ads for unhealthy food shouldn't be allowed when children are most likely to be watching TV.
> Three in four parents think the way that foods are marketed to children makes it more difficult to get them to eat healthily.
> Nearly 9 out of 10 parents think food companies need to be more responsible in the way they market food to children.

PRESS RELEASE

Embargoed until 00:01hrs Friday 9 March 2007
Contact Joe Bloggs on 020 123 1234 or joe bloggs@which.co.uk

Could try harder...

Two years ago the Government launched its Food and Health Action Plan to improve public health and encourage healthy eating. Two years on, Which? reports on its progress in four key areas:

1. Simplified Food Labelling

Several food retailers and manufacturers have adopted the Food Standard Agency's traffic light labelling scheme but many have simply ignored it. Robust research confirms its usefulness and the Government must do more to encourage others to follow suit. Trying hard but underachieving.
9/10 for effort, but just 6/10 for achievement

2. Food advertising and promotion to children

The Government has still not published clear success criteria for action in this area. Ofcom's timetable on TV advertising restrictions has severely slipped and its final proposals will have a limited effect. There has been little progress for tackling other forms of non-broadcast promotions. Extremely disappointing performance.
Scores 5/10 for effort and only 3/10 for achievement

3. Working with the food industry to reduce fat, sugar and salt

Although targets for salt consumption were published in March 2006, targets for sugar, fat and portion targets are still undecided. More progress is crucial in this area. A good start, but it's now time for less talk and more action.
Scores 8/10 for effort but only 3/10 for achievement

4. School meals

Secondary and primary school standards on the nutritional content of school meals were delivered in time. These are robust measures but must now be monitored closely. Excellent progress made and a gold star for effort.
Scores 10/10 for effort and 7/10 for achievement

Sue Davies, chief policy adviser, Which? says:

"Although the Government is trying hard, it is still underachieving and failing to reach its own targets. School meals are the star pupil but we need real progress in the other areas."

which
?

Notes to editors

The Food and Health Action Plan brought together all Government action targets
relating to food and nutrition from the Choosing Health White Paper – published in 2005.

A PDF of Which?'s report card for the Government's Food and Health Action Plan is
attached. Please contact the press office (0123 456 7890) if you cannot open this and a
faxed copy can be sent through.

APPENDIX 4

A local campaigner's guide to the planning system

This guide has been written by Gay Brown. A full version appears on the Tescopoly website (www.tescopoly.org). It has been adapted with Gay's help.

Gay has been campaign co-ordinator representing residents and traders of Yiewsley in West London who have been fighting against a huge out-of-town Tesco superstore since 1994.

- Know your rights. Remember, as locals you're entitled to information (e.g. the council and the developer are required to involve locals 'at the earliest possible point' under Planning Policy Statement 6). Both council and developer have to produce a 'statement of community involvement' – see later.

- Start a petition. Consider a planning hearing in London where each petition you submit will get you a slot of around five minutes to address the planning meeting. This is common practice, but do check. You probably only need around 25 signatures for a petition, but check with your local authority. Big petitions sound good in the press, but lots of little ones will probably do more good. You might need at least six slots to put forward a case at a planning hearing. Start your petition as follows, 'Please add your name and details to this petition if you wish to support our objection to the plans for a new...' For more information on petitions, see chapter 4.

- Write to councillors. You can find out who the chair of the planning committee is and which councillors sit on the committee and then mailshot all the councillors explaining each of your objections properly. Make sure you include the committee secretary and ask if they can distribute to all committee members.

- Prepare your case. If you are able to speak at a council meeting, prepare your arguments and statement carefully. As mentioned above, if you and your supporters all stand up and say the same thing you probably won't get all your objections aired, plus you're not going to look professional and you'll waste everyone's time.

- Read the plans for the development. You need to see the plans and any officer's report that has been prepared for the meeting. You're entitled to a copy of every document that the developers submit. Go to the reception of your council's planning department and ask to speak to the planning officer responsible for the application. They will be writing the officer's report. This is usually available less than two weeks before the meeting at which it will be considered. Try to ensure that you get a copy of this report at the earliest possible opportunity. Arrange to collect it from the council offices – this could save you a couple of days. You may also be able to get the information online, but some councils are better than others at posting such documents on their websites.

- Seek to influence the council officer dealing with your concern. Judge the scale of opposition (include petitions and letters from MPs, ward councillors, local residents, tenants and retailers). Make the opposition sound as substantial as possible by grouping, for example, all retailers on one road or all residents on one estate together on one petition. One effective method is to get each local retailer to raise a petition for you. Take the petitions in by hand and make sure you get a receipt for each one. They often get 'lost' in council offices.

- Obtain all the relevant local, regional and national planning legislation from the council. You're entitled to hard copies. The old Unitary Development Plans are being replaced by Local Development Frameworks (in other words, the framework that local councils are required to put together detailing planning policy for the area). There are also regional planning documents. Build an argument. There are numerous grounds for objecting to an application – such as loss of jobs, noise, vibration, traffic congestion, delivery lorries, pollution and consultation (or lack of) (see chapter 7).

• Have you been consulted? For many council matters the local authority has a duty to consult with the community. Ask how the council has consulted. The developer and the council will have to produce a 'statement of community involvement' to show how they've made their plans known – this is usually a 'tick box' exercise. Consultation is a two-way process and just putting a leaflet through the door doesn't count. Public meetings need to be checked out and attendance records counted. You should also see the file of responses sent to the council on the development and read each letter. Check all petitions that do not come from your group and see if you can persuade the other groups to join forces. It's useful to know where your opposition might come from.

• The statement of community involvement has to be a genuine two-way process. In reality it is often a tick box exercise. However, it is vital for campaigners because a lack of consultation can be reason enough to turn down an application.

• Write to all councillors and all members of the planning committee about two weeks ahead of the planning meeting. Outline your objections. Use bullet points, be precise and back up your arguments with evidence. Quote the Unitary Development Plans or Local Development Frameworks for each piece of evidence.

• Remember you pay the wages of council officers. You are entitled to as many meetings as the developer has had. Ask council staff to explain the documents to you until you are satisfied with their explanation.

Model Freedom of Information letters

These letter templates can be adapted for most Freedom of Information requests. As mentioned in chapter 7 requests under the Freedom of Information Act, the Environmental Information Regulations, and the Data Protection Act do not have to mention the specific legislation itself. Sometimes it might be easier to just call up and ask for the information instead. These letters are for those instances when a more formal approach is needed.

These letters are taken from the book *Your Right to Know* by Heather Brooke (2007, Pluto Press) and are reproduced by the kind permission of the author and her publisher. For further information see Heather Brooke's website, www.yrtk.org.

FREEDOM OF INFORMATION LETTER 1 (general)

[Your address]
[Your daytime telephone number]
[Your email address]

Freedom of Information Officer
[Name of organisation]
[Organisation's address]

[Insert date]

Dear [enter name]

I am writing to request information under the Freedom of Information Act 2000. In order to assist you with this request, I am outlining my query as specifically as possible.

[Give a description of request]

I would be interested in any information held by your organisation regarding my request. I understand that I do not have to specify particular files or documents and that it is the department's responsibility to provide the information I require. If you need further clarification, please contact me by [preferred contact method, i.e. phone, email, post].

I would like to receive the information in [specify your chosen format here: electronic, hard copy, and/or to inspect the documents on-site].

If my request is denied in whole or in part, I ask that you justify all deletions by reference to specific exemptions of the Act. I will also expect you to release all non-exempt material. I reserve the right to appeal your decision to withhold any information to charge excessive fees.

I would be grateful if you could confirm in writing that you have received this request. I look forward to your response within 20 working days, as outlined by the statute.

Regards

[Your name]

FREEDOM OF INFORMATION LETTER 2 (commercial)

[Your address]
[Your daytime telephone number]
[Your email address]

Freedom of Information Officer
[Name of organisation]
[Organisation's address]

[Insert date]

Dear [enter name]

I would like to request the following information.

1. The contract (including all indexes, appendices and supplements) between the [name of public authority] and [the private company]; (and/or)
2. Bids to tender for [specify service or project]; (and/or)
3. The annual revenue [public authority] receives from [private company] as a result of this contract.

I would like to receive the information in [specify your chosen format here: electronic, hard copy, and/or to inspect the documents on-site]. If one part of this request can be answered sooner than others, please send that information first followed by any subsequent data. If you need further clarification, please contact me by [state your preferred contact method, i.e. phone, email, post].

Many public authorities release their contracts with private vendors in line with the Freedom of Information Act. The exemption for commercial interest under the Act (section 43) is a qualified exemption, which means information can only be withheld if it is in the public's interest. The public have an interest in knowing the terms of the contracts awarded by public authorities, whether or not public money changes hands immediately.

If you are relying on section 41 (the exemption for legal breach of confidence) I would like to know the following:

• When these confidentiality agreements were agreed.
• All correspondence and email in which these confidentiality agreements were discussed.
• The precise wording of the confidentiality agreements.

I ask these questions because guidance issued by both the Lord

Chancellor (draft guidance on FOI implementation) and the Office of Government Commerce (model terms and conditions for goods and services) specifically state that public authorities should not enter into these types of agreements; they go directly against the spirit of the laws of disclosure. I would also point to the Information Commissioner's guidance on accepting blanket commercial confidentiality agreements, 'unless confidentiality clauses are necessary or reasonable, there is a real risk that, in the event of a complaint, the Commissioner would order disclosure in any case.'[1]

Finally, within the law of confidence there is also a public interest test. Therefore the contracts should be disclosed in full. If any parts are redacted they must be for information that can be proven to be a legal breach of confidence in court, and only then where secrecy can be shown to be in the public interest. These are difficult positions to argue when public money is at stake or where a public authority is offering a private company a monopoly to charge its stakeholders.

I reserve the right to appeal your decision to withhold any information or to charge excessive fees, and understand that under the Act, I am entitled to a response within 20 working days. I would be grateful if you could confirm in writing that you have received this request.

Regards

[Your name]

---

[1] Freedom of Information Awareness Guidance 5 – www.informationcommissioner.gov.uk/eventual.aspx?id=102

FREEDOM OF INFORMATION LETTER 3 (appeal)

[Your address]
[Your daytime telephone number]
[Your email address]

Agency Director or Appeal Officer
[Name of organisation]
[Organisation's address]

[Insert date]

Re: Freedom of Information Act Appeal

Dear [enter name]

I would like to appeal your organisation's refusal to positively answer my request for information made [insert date of request] under the Freedom of Information Act 2000.

My request was assigned the following reference number: [insert reference number]. On [insert date of denial], I received a response to my request from [insert name of official] who denied my request. Under the terms of the Freedom of Information Act, I am exercising my right to seek an internal review of this decision.

[Optional] The documents that were withheld should be disclosed under the Freedom of Information Act because [they do not meet the exception criteria and/or disclosure is in the public interest – make your argument about why the public interest favours disclosure (see chapter 7)].

[Optional] I appeal this decision to require me to pay [insert fee amount here] in fees for this request as the information I requested is in the public interest and the information should therefore be easily accessible to the public. The Freedom of Information Act states that an authority can only charge 'reasonable' fees and this amount is unreasonable. If the fee decision is upheld, I require a full breakdown of how the total amount was calculated and a justification of how this amount can be considered 'reasonable'.

Thank you for consideration of this appeal.

Regards

[Your name]

FREEDOM OF INFORMATION LETTER 4 (environmental)

[Your address]
[Your daytime telephone number]
[Your email address]

Agency Director or Freedom of Information Officer
[Name of organisation]
[Organisation's address]

[Insert date]

Dear [enter name]

I am writing to request information under the Environmental Information Regulations 2004/Freedom of Information Act 2000. In order to assist you with this request, I am outlining my query as specifically as possible.

[Give a description of your request here]

I would be interested in any information held by your organisation regarding my request. I understand that I do not have to specify particular files or documents and that it is the department's responsibility to provide the information I require. If you need further clarification, please contact me by [state your preferred contact method, e.g. phone, email, post].

I would like to receive the information in [specify your chosen format here: electronic, hard copy, and/or to inspect the documents on-site].

If my request is denied in whole or in part, I ask that you justify all deletions by reference to specific exemptions of the Act. I will also expect you to release all non-exempt material. I reserve the right to appeal your decision to withhold any information or to charge excessive fees. If you plan to charge a fee for this information, I would ask that you pay particular attention to the ruling on fees made by the Information Tribunal 28 March 2006: *Mr David Markinson v Information Commissioner.*

This decision makes clear that public authorities cannot charge an unreasonable amount for environmental information. It directed King's Lynn and West Norfolk Borough Council to overturn their charging structure and adopt instead a price of 10p per photocopied A4 page. Section 44 of the Tribunal decision states that a public authority can only exceed the guide price if it can demonstrate a good reason to do so, and in considering whether any such reason exists the public authority should:

i. take due regard of the guidance set out in the Code of Practice on the discharge of the obligations of public authorities under the Environmental Information Regulations 2004 and the Guidance to the Environmental Information Regulations 2004, both published by Defra, to the effect that any charge should be at a level that does not exceed the cost of producing the copies;

ii. disregard any costs, including staff costs, associated with the maintenance of the information in question or its identification or extraction of storage; and

iii. disregard any factors beyond the number and size of sheets to be copied, in particular, the real or perceived significance of the content, or the effect that any charging structure may have on the council's revenue or its staff workload.

I look forward to your response within the 20 working-day time limit, and would be grateful if you could confirm in writing that you have received this request.

Regards

[Your name]

APPENDIX 6

The text below comes from the civil liberties group Liberty. This advice is frequently updated because of the changing nature of public order laws and the most recent information can be found on its online guide to human rights, www.YourRights.org.uk. The advice below was prepared in 2007. The authors are grateful to Pluto Press for allowing them to reproduce this information. For more details about Pluto Press please see their website at www.plutobooks.com.

Your Right to Peaceful Protest

If you are organising a public meeting in the local pub, a march down the high street on a busy Saturday afternoon, or a demo outside the town hall, you need to be aware of what you can and can't do under the law. Peaceful protest was only introduced by the Human Rights Act. As Liberty points out, that right is not absolute and there are a number of laws that can effectively curtail your rights. The recent concern of politicians with anti-social behaviour as well as the threat of terrorism means that right has been weakened while at the same time the police have been given greater powers to restrict the actions of demonstrators. The following has been adapted from Liberty's Guide *Your Right to Peaceful Protest.*

Are you holding a public meeting?

A public meeting is one that is open to the public to attend, with or without payment, and is held in a public place. Private premises, including town halls and council buildings, church halls, pubs, become 'public places' when public meetings are held there. If you are the organiser, you must ensure that you comply with the terms and conditions for the use of the premises, including fire and safety regulations, and that the meeting is conducted in an orderly manner. Stewards should be easily identifiable, but they should not wear a uniform to promote a political objective or signify membership of a political organisation. They must not try to take over the functions of the police or use force to promote a political objective (these acts would be illegal). They can assist in the admission and seating of members of the public and in the control of disorder or to remove members of the public who go too far in their heckling.

It is an offence (under the Public Meeting Act 1908) to try to break up a lawful public meeting by acting in a disorderly manner or to incite others to do so. The maximum penalty is six months' imprisonment and/or a fine up to £1000. If a police officer is present and reasonably suspects you of trying to disrupt the meeting, then, at the chairperson's request, he or she can ask you for your name and address. It is an offence if you fail to give these details or give a false name or address (maximum penalty is a fine at level 1 – currently £200).

If there is serious disruption or aggression, and if the police believe that you are involved, then, relying on their common law powers to prevent a breach of the peace, the police could ask you to leave the meeting, threatening you with arrest if you refused, or they could arrest you for an offence under the Public Order Act 1986 (POA).

Any meeting of two or more people that is wholly or partly in the open air is a 'public assembly' and subject to conditions imposed by the police under the POA. If such a meeting is attended by 20 or more people and held on land without the owner's permission it may be a 'trespassory assembly' – see later – and could be subject to a banning order. Organisers should be aware that plain clothes police officers might attend political meetings without authority for the purpose of collecting information.

Election Meetings

The Representation of the People Act 1983 makes special provision for public meetings held at the time of local or national elections. All candidates are entitled to use rooms in local schools and other publicly owned meeting halls, free of charge, for election meetings provided that the meetings are open to the public and are intended to further the candidates' prospects by discussion of election issues. Some local authorities have refused permission to the National Front to use their premises for election meetings on the grounds that the National Front did not intend their meetings to be genuinely open to the public or because damage was likely to be caused to the premises. The 1983 Act makes it an offence, punishable with a fine up to level 5 (currently £5,000), to disrupt, or to incite others to disrupt an election meeting. If a police officer reasonably suspects you of trying to disrupt the meeting, then, at the chairperson's request, he or she can ask you for your name and address and it is an offence if you fail to give these details or falsify them (maximum penalty is a fine at level 1 – currently £200). Police powers for public meetings also apply to election meetings.

Are you holding a private meeting?

A meeting is private if members of the public are not free to attend, paying or otherwise (for example the meeting of a trade union branch or a political party). A private meeting remains private even though it is held in a public building such as a town hall. Organisers can refuse entry or require someone to leave. Private meetings are governed by the rules of the organisation involved, or by conditions specified by the organisers together with any requirements, for example, as to maximum numbers, which apply to the premises where the meeting takes place. Unless the organisers invite the police, they have no right to enter a private meeting and can be asked to leave unless they are present to prevent crime or an imminent breach of the peace.

Are you planning a march?

The POA refers to marches as 'processions' and to all other static demonstrations as 'assemblies'. A 'procession' is simply defined as people moving together along a route. The law does not provide a minimum number to constitute a procession, so even a handful of people going to a town hall to hand in a petition will constitute a procession. The POA gives the police extensive controls over processions. Organisers must give advance notice to the police. The police may impose conditions on processions and, in limited circumstances, have them banned. Failure to comply with these provisions is a criminal offence.

Who is the organiser?

There is no legal definition. For a big procession an official organiser will probably have been selected well in advance of the date. For an informal event the organiser could be anyone who takes the lead. Some spontaneous events will have no organiser.

Do you need to give advance notice?

The rules are designed to ensure that the police are told, in advance, about the vast majority of 'political' marches. Specifically, they say that notice should be given of any procession if it is intended to:

- demonstrate support for or opposition to the views or actions of any group;
- publicise a cause or campaign; and
- mark or commemorate an event.

Notice need not be given if it is not reasonably practicable to do so in advance. This is intended to allow for a completely spontaneous procession. If a prosecution is brought, it will be for the Magistrates' Court to decide whether notice of any kind could have been given. A last-minute telephone call to the police is advisable to show you are prepared to follow the spirit of the law. A record should be kept of the call.

Where notice is required it must be in writing and must include:

- the date of the procession;
- the time it will start;

- the proposed route; and
- the name and the address of the organiser.

The written notice must be delivered to a police station in the area where the procession is planned to start, either by hand or by recorded delivery six clear days in advance – for example, on Saturday for a procession the following Saturday. If a procession is planned at short notice (less than one week), then the organiser is required to deliver written notice by hand as soon as reasonably practicable.

The organiser commits an offence if:

- notice was not given as required; or
- the date, starting time or route differs from the notice.

In practice, in the handful of prosecutions brought under the POA, it has proved very difficult for the police to prove that a particular person was the organiser of a march. Unless the police can do so, their powers to prosecute are greatly curtailed. Even if they can, it is a defence if you can prove either:

- you were not aware that notice had not been given or not given in time; or
- the different date, starting time or route was due to circumstances beyond your control or was changed with the agreement of the police or by direction of the police.

The police have extensive powers to impose conditions on marches, even to ban them. In advance, the Chief Constable (or the Metropolitan Police Commissioner in London) can impose conditions relating to the route, number of marchers, types of banners or duration, or restrict entry to a public place. These conditions must be in writing. After the procession has begun the most senior officer on the spot can impose similar conditions, which do not have to be in writing. The POA says that conditions can be imposed only if the senior officer reasonably believes that the procession may result in:

- serious public disorder; or

- serious damage to property; or

- serious disruption to the life of the community.

The senior officer may also impose conditions if he or she reasonably believes that the purpose of the organisers is to intimidate others 'with a view to compelling them not to do an act they have a right to do, or to do an act they have a right not to do'. The conditions must be ones that the officer believes are necessary to prevent disorder, damage, disruption or intimidation. Where organisers have sufficient notice of proposed conditions, they can be challenged in the courts.

Can the police ban our march? The POA gives police power to ban all or a 'class' of processions in a local area for up to three months by way of a banning order. If a Chief Constable (or the Commissioner in London) is satisfied that the powers to impose conditions will not be sufficient to prevent serious public disorder if the procession takes place, then he must apply for a banning order.

Are you planning a demo?

Unlike public processions, there is normally no requirement to give prior notice of an assembly but, under the POA, the police do have specific powers to control assemblies. Two persons can constitute an 'assembly'. A public place is any highway (including the pavement) and any other place to which the public or a section of the public can have access.

The senior police officer at the scene has the power to impose conditions but only if he or she reasonably believes that:

- the conditions are necessary to prevent serious public disorder, serious damage to property or serious disruption to the life of the community; or

- the purpose of the person organising the assembly is to intimidate others.

The only conditions that may be imposed on a public assembly under POA are on:

- location;
- maximum number of people; and
- maximum duration of the assembly.

Note also that although the police have power to impose conditions, there is no power to ban a public assembly altogether. Therefore, if the conditions are so strict that they in effect prohibit the assembly from taking effect in any meaningful way (such as if the conditions restrict the protest to five people, in a side street away from the public and for a maximum of five minutes), it may be that they amount to a ban and are unlawful. An attempt by the police to impose excessively strict conditions may also be a breach of the protesters' rights to assembly under the European Convention on Human Rights.

What if you are holding a demo near Parliament?

Different rules apply. The Serious Organised Crime and Police Act 2005 introduced new restrictions. If you want to conduct a 'demonstration' in the 'designated area' you must give written notice to the Metropolitan Police Commissioner stating the date and time when the demonstration is to be carried out, how it is to be carried out, and whether it is to be carried out by him/herself or not. The notice must, if reasonably practicable, be given not less than six clear days before the day on which the demonstration is to start, or if not reasonably practicable, as soon as it is, and in any event, not less than 24 hours before the time the demonstration is to start.

A 'demonstration' is not defined but it is possible for one person to carry out a 'demonstration' on his or her own. For example, a lone woman reading the names of the soldiers killed in Iraq was held to constitute a 'demonstration'. However, processions which require notification under section 11 of the POA (see Marches and Processions) are not covered by this provision. The designated area is a large area around Parliament that includes all of Whitehall, some parts of the Southbank, as well as Westminster and Parliament Square itself. Trafalgar Square is not included in the designated area.

The Commissioner must give authorisation if the required notice is given but he may impose conditions if these are necessary to prevent:

- serious public disorder;
- serious damage to property;
- disruption to the life of the community;
- risk to security or to health and safety; and
- hindrance to the proper operation of Parliament or to any person wishing to leave or enter Parliament.

So in the designated area the police have greater powers to impose conditions as, unlike demos elsewhere, there is no need for there to be a risk of serious disruption to the life of the community but merely a risk of disruption or of hindrance. Any demonstration will be likely to cause some level of disruption or hindrance. In addition the conditions that can be imposed are broader: in addition to number, location and duration, the conditions can relate to size of banners and noise levels or any other such conditions that the Commissioner considers necessary. In addition, loudspeaker or loudhailers are banned within the designated area completely.

If a demonstration is carried out in the designated area without authorisation, both the organisers and the participants will be guilty of an offence. It is also an offence to knowingly fail to comply with a condition which is imposed on the demonstrators, although there is a defence if the demonstrator can show that the failure to comply with the condition arose from circumstances beyond his or her control.

If you are holding a demo or a march...

The law provides a specific right to use a public highway and peaceful assemblies that do not prevent other people from also using the highway are likely to be seen as 'reasonable use'. In addition, the

European Convention on Human Rights guarantees the right to assembly, so you have a positive right both under domestic law and European legislation.

However, unreasonable obstruction of the highway is a criminal offence. This is a widely drawn offence, so the police have often seen it in practice as a licensing power over public gatherings and use it to remove sit-down demonstrators, to keep marchers from leaving the agreed police route, to control pickets and in every conceivable public order context on the highway. Often the police will give a warning to move before making an arrest, although there is no legal requirement to do so. However, if you were not given a warning that you were causing an obstruction, it will be easier to show that you were not making unreasonable use of the highway.

The offence is obstructing the highway, not other highway users. So it is not necessary to prove that any other person was actually obstructed. In practice the offence turns on whether a particular obstruction was reasonable rather than whether there was, in fact, an obstruction. The test of reasonableness is always objective. Was there an actual obstruction? If there was, how long did it last? Where was it? What was its purpose?

Because there is a positive right to use the highway for reasonable purposes, the test of reasonableness can very often be argued successfully in demonstration cases, particularly where the police have taken no action in the past or where the obstruction was trivial. In practice, it is often very helpful to have photographs to show just how extensive – or limited – a particular obstruction was.

The offence can be tried in the Magistrates' Court only. The maximum penalty is a fine up to level 3 (currently £1,000). There is no power to send a person convicted of highway obstruction to prison.

Also consider local by-laws. By-laws for parks may, for example, prohibit public meetings, bill-posting, the erection of notices, stalls and booths, and the sale or distribution of pamphlets and leaflets.

They will usually give the police and local authority officials the power to remove anybody who breaches the by-laws. A copy of local by-laws should be on sale at the local town hall and also available for inspection. It is an offence to breach a by-law and the penalty is usually set out in the particular by-law.

Protests on private land

The right to assembly generally only applies in public places. If you protest on private land without the permission of the occupier, you will be trespassing. Trespassing is not normally a criminal offence but a tort (or civil wrong). This means that the occupier can sue the trespasser, or apply for a court order for possession, but the police cannot normally arrest someone merely because they are trespassing. However, recent changes in the law have created new criminal offences connected with trespass.

Aggravated Trespass

The offence of 'aggravated trespass' is committed when a person trespasses on land when a lawful activity is taking place on that land or land nearby and he or she does anything intending to intimidate, obstruct or disrupt that activity.

Trespassory assemblies

Under the Public Order Act 1986, if a chief police officer reasonably believes that there is a risk of 'trespassory assemblies' that will result in serious disruption to the life of the community or in damage to important buildings or monuments in a particular area, he can apply to the local council for an order prohibiting all such assemblies. This provision was added to the POA in the 1990s to deal with 'raves' and 'new age' groups celebrating the solstice in Stonehenge. A 'trespassory assembly' is 20 or more people on land in the open air without the permission, or in excess of the permission, of the occupier. The police will also have the power to stop persons whom they reasonably believe are going to a trespassory assembly and to direct them not to proceed. Failure to obey such a direction is an offence.

Trespass on designated sites

The Serious Organised Crime and Police Act 2005 created the new offence of trespassing on a designated site. This was introduced as intending to deal with protesters that trespassed on Royal properties, such as the Fathers4Justice protesters that climbed up Buckingham Palace. However, in addition to Crown land, this section also allows the Secretary of State to designate any other site which he considers appropriate to designate in the interests of national security. There is no definition of national security – the Secretary of State could designate, for example, embassies, arms fairs, military bases, or government buildings. So far the type of locations that have been designated have been military bases. The offence is that of entering or being on any designated site as a trespasser. It is a defence if the person charged can prove that he did not know, and had no reasonable cause to suspect that the site was designated.

Criminal Damage

It is an offence under the Criminal Damage Act 1971 if you damage or destroy property or threaten to do so intentionally or recklessly and without lawful excuse.

Are you planning a picket?

In recent years, picketing has been used by campaigning groups as an effective way of bringing their views to public attention, for example, by picketing premises where politicians are due to attend, demonstrating outside head offices of organisations and 'blockading' ports and airports supporting live animal exports. The law gives special status to picketing when it is related to an industrial dispute, but no special exemption under the criminal law. However, most picketing is lawful unless it causes an obstruction of the highway or is designed to intimidate.

You are protected under the civil law if you picket in connection with an industrial dispute at or near your workplace for the purpose of peacefully obtaining or communicating information or peacefully persuading any person to work or abstain from working

(Trade Union and Labour Relations Act 1992). Employers have increasingly used the civil courts to get injunctions in order to limit the effectiveness of picketing. Injunctions have been granted on the basis that it was not the workplace of some or all of the pickets, or that the picketing was not peaceful. Unions that continue to picket in breach of an injunction are in contempt of court and liable to pay very heavy fines. By injunction the court can limit the location and number of pickets and impose conditions on their conduct.

Secondary picketing – picketing at a workplace or premises where you do not work – does not have the same civil law protection, but is not a criminal offence. It is worth remembering that the police do not have any enhanced powers over secondary pickets and it is not their job to enforce the civil law on picketing, even if an injunction is in force. Their general powers in this area are dealt with below.

Police powers and picketing

Giving the police greater power to control and restrict picketing was a primary purpose of the POA. Any picket of two or more people is a 'public assembly' and therefore subject to police conditions under the POA. In addition to the power to impose conditions, the police possess a wide range of public order powers to restrict and control picketing and to arrest pickets for various offences. These include:

- obstruction of the highway on the basis of too many pickets, even if they are moving, or a single picket trying to compel a driver to stop and listen;

- obstruction of the police;

- using threatening, abusive or insulting words or behaviour;

- disorderly conduct likely to cause harassment, alarm or distress; and

- aggravated trespass.

Can I leaflet, collect money or put up posters?

Generally speaking, the law allows wider latitude for collecting money for charitable operations than for commercial or political ones, both of which are more closely regulated by licensing. 'Charitable purposes' means any charitable, benevolent or philanthropic purpose. It includes the relief of poverty and the advancement of religion or education at home or abroad, but it does not include collections to raise funds for a political party or for a political campaign, such as CND or animal liberation. However, the law relating to these subjects is confused and inconsistently applied by the police. If in doubt, check by-laws with the local authority and the police beforehand.

There is no need to obtain a licence or certificate for handing out leaflets or collecting signatures for a petition. A leaflet must have on it the name and address of the printer. Some by-laws contain restrictions on the places where leafleting may take place; check the by-laws at the town hall. The police may also move leafleters if they appear to be causing an obstruction. It is an offence to hand out leaflets that are threatening, abusive or insulting, or those that are intended to stir up racial hatred.

A petition to Parliament is governed by special rules and must conform to special wording. Copies of the rules can be obtained from the House of Commons.

Sticking up posters in public places is quite legal, so long as:

- you have the consent of the owner of the hoarding, fence or wall in question;
- the poster is no more than six feet square;
- it advertises a non-commercial event, including political, educational or social meetings;
- there is no by-law to prevent it.

Persons over 18 may sell newspapers in the street or from door-to-door, as long as the sale is for campaigning purposes. If the sale is for profit, it becomes street trading or peddling (if door-to-door), both of which are illegal without a licence. Sometimes difficulty is caused because the police believe that the newspaper or magazine is less of a campaigning document and more a device to raise money for a political organisation. Also, the sale of newspapers may obstruct the highway, which is a criminal offence.

APPENDIX 7

Useful addresses

Campaign for Freedom of
Information
Suite 102
16 Baldwins Gardens
London EC1N 7RJ
Tel: 020 7831 7477
admin@cfoi.demon.co.uk
www.cfoi.org.uk

Campaign to Protect Rural
England
CPRE National Office
128 Southwark Street
London SE1 0SW
Tel: 020 7981 2800
info@cpre.org.uk
www.cpre.org.uk

Charity Commission
Charity Commission Direct
PO Box 1227
Liverpool L69 3UG
Tel: 0845 3000 218
www.charity-
commission.gov.uk

Civic Trust
Essex Hall
1–6 Essex Street
London WC2R 3HU
Tel: 020 7539 7900
info@civictrust.org.uk
www.civictrust.org.uk

Companies House
Crown Way
Maindy
Cardiff CF14 3UZ
Tel: 0870 33 33 636
enquiries@companies-
house.gov.uk
www.companieshouse.gov.uk

Environmental Law Foundation
Suite 309
16 Baldwins Gardens
London EC1N 7RJ
Tel: 020 7404 1030
info@elflaw.org
www.elflaw.org

Friends of the Earth
26–28 Underwood Street
London N1 7JQ
Tel: 020 7490 1555
www.foe.co.uk

Help the Aged
207–221 Pentonville Road
London N1 9UZ
Tel: 020 7278 1114
info@helptheaged.org.uk
www.helptheaged.org.uk

Information Commissioner's
Office
Wycliffe House
Water Lane
Wilmslow
Cheshire SK9 5AF
Tel: 08456 30 60 60/ 01625 54
57 45
mail@ico.gsi.gov.uk.
www.ico.gov.uk

Institute of Fundraising
Park Place
12 Lawn Lane
London SW8 1UD
Tel: 020 7840 1000
www.institute-of-
fundraising.org.uk

Law Society
113 Chancery Lane
London WC2A 1PL
Tel: 020 7242 1222
contact@lawsociety.org.uk
www.lawsociety.org.uk

Legal Action Group
242 Pentonville Road
London N1 9UN
Tel: 020 7833 2931
lag@lag.org.uk
www.lag.org.uk

Legal Services Commission
85 Gray's Inn Road
London WC1X 8TX
Tel: 0845 345 4 345
(Community Legal Advice
helpline)
www.legalservices.gov.uk

Liberty
21 Tabard Street
London SE1 4LA
Tel: 020 7403 3888
www.liberty-human-
rights.org.uk

Local Government Association
Local Government House
Smith Square
London SW1P 3HZ
Tel: 020 7664 3131
info@lga.gov.uk
www.lga.gov.uk

Market Research Society
15 Northburgh Street
London EC1V 0JR
Tel: 020 7490 4911
info@mrs.org.uk
www.mrs.org.uk

Ministry of Justice
Selborne House
54 Victoria Street
London SW1E 6QW
Tel: 020 7210 8500
www.justice.gov.uk

National Council for Voluntary
Organisations
Regent's Wharf
8 All Saints Street
London N1 9RL
Tel: 0800 2 798 798 (helpline)
helpdesk@askncvo.org.uk
www.ncvo-vol.org.uk

Oxfam
Oxfam House
John Smith Drive
Cowley
Oxford OX4 2JY
Tel: 0870 333 2700
www.oxfam.org.uk

Public Law Project
150 Caledonian Road
London N1 9RD
Tel: 020 7697 2190
admin@publiclawproject.org.uk
www.publiclawproject.org.uk

Sheila McKechnie Foundation
Marylebone Road
London NW1 4DF
Tel: 020 7770 7892
www.sheilamckechnie.org.uk

Surfers Against Sewage
Unit 2
Wheal Kitty Workshops
St Agnes
Cornwall TR5 0RD
Tel: 01872 555950
www.sas.org.uk

Which?
Castlemead
Gascoyne Way
Hertford SG14 1LH
Tel: 01992 822800
which@which.co.uk
www.which.co.uk

Xtraordinary People
(British Dyslexia Association)
Unit 8, Bracknell Beeches
Old Bracknell Lane
Bracknell RG12 7BW
Tel: 01344 381565
info@xtraordinarypeople.com
www.xtraordinarypeople.com

INDEX